Twenty-five 5-MINUTE POWER SCENES

Lena Harris

The Lena Harris Studio
Beverly Hills, California

In E-Z Read® Format

Scene Study Series

A Smith and Kraus Book

A Smith and Kraus Book
Published by Smith and Kraus, Inc.
177 Lyme Road, Hanover, NH 03755
www.smithandkraus.com

Manufactured in the United States of America

Cover Photograph of Lena Harris © 2005 by Gary Bernstein
Cover and Text Design by Julia Hill Gignoux

First Edition: November 2005
10 9 8 7 6 5 4 3 2 1

Library of Congress Cataloging-in-Publication Data
Harris, Lena.
25 five-minute power scenes / Lena Harris. —1st ed.
p. cm. — (Scene study series)
ISBN 1-57525-432-8
1. Dialogues. 2. Acting. I. Title: Twenty-five five-minute power scenes. II. Title. III. Series.

PN2080.H37 2005
812'.6—dc22
2005054140

To my wonderful family, Gary, Romé, and Caron.
I love you.

Special thanks to my actors.

Contents

Introduction

As an acting teacher and coach, and in my work with the studios, I have found a desperate need for short, contemporary scenes that are universal and not limited by age or nationality—scenes that provide an extreme range of emotions, actions, and impediments and that give the actor a complete workout.

I have spent endless hours reading plays and scripts, only to end up cutting and pasting the scenes together in an effort to provide the needed material. Ultimately, I found it to be more efficient and pragmatic to write the scenes myself.

My scenes are used in a variety of ways. In my Audition Technique Workshop for example, the actors are given the same scene. They have an hour to memorize the scene and apply their tools and techniques; after which, I direct the scene and videotape the actors as though they were auditioning for a casting director. In the real world, actors typically receive their scripts a day before the audition. Consequently, this exercise is a "muscle-building" workout. The scenes may also be used as part of the actor's reel.

Additionally, actors use these scenes for showcasing and for auditioning for agents (and managers). The agents often request that actors prepare scenes in addition to monologues, the reason being that uninformed or overzealous actors sometimes direct their monologue performance to the agent, even though the agent is not a character within the monologue. Doing this immediately creates problems. The agent becomes uncomfortable because he or she has unwittingly been forced to become part of the monologue, and as such, the agent is unable to observe the actor's performance.

Notwithstanding the importance of a monologue, only the performance of a scene enables the agent to observe the connectedness between the actors, the specificity of their relationships, and the use of the behavior.

Most agents request both a short comedy scene and a dramatic scene. Therefore I present a variety of each for this book, to best express each actor's talent and uniqueness.

Lena Harris
Beverly Hills, California

ALLY

(1 male/1 female, drama)

BREAKDOWN Danny and Betty are lovers and married to other people. Betty is now four months pregnant with Danny's child. Danny had promised to leave his wife, Sarah, six months ago, but she was in a car accident, resulting in the death of their three-year-old child.

SETTING The bedroom of Betty's apartment. Danny and Betty have spent the afternoon together making love.

• • •

(Betty enters the bedroom from the bathroom closing the clasp on her necklace.)

DANNY: Come here.

BETTY: No.

DANNY: What's the matter?

BETTY: *(Pouting.)* I don't want this day to end.

DANNY: Me either. Come here.

(Betty goes to the mirror, arranges her hair, and puts the finishing touches on her makeup.)

DANNY: You are some beauty. You know that? Every inch of you.

BETTY: *(Coyly.)* Oh . . . surely you jest.

DANNY: Come here!

(Betty whirls around as if to model her outfit. Danny applauds. They both laugh, and he pulls her down beside him.)

DANNY: I love you! I think I may even worship you . . . I know how lucky I am. I am . . .

BETTY: I love you too . . .

(They start to kiss. Betty stops suddenly upon hearing a noise out-side the door. She freezes. Danny starts to speak, and she quickly puts her finger over his lips to hush him. They both freeze and look at each other. Betty tiptoes slowly to the door, turns back to Danny, puts her finger over her lips to make sure he doesn't speak. She looks carefully through the peephole in the door and sees a cat.)

BETTY: It's a stupid CAT!

DANNY: Why are you so uptight? I thought Claude wasn't due back in town until Saturday.

BETTY: HE'S NOT! I'm just jumpy—that's all.

DANNY: Well, I almost had a heart attack! You've gotta calm down! It's not good for the baby either.

BETTY: I know. I'm sorry! I can't live like this! I can't stand to be in the same room with him . . . especially now. I know he senses something. Suddenly, he's all interested in . . . Fortunately, he drinks so much he passes out . . . before . . . anything happens. I hate him! He's a monster. Danny, I thought we would be together by now.

(There is a pause. Danny lowers his head. He is thinking about the death of his child. Betty continues.)

BETTY: I'm sorry . . . I am so sorry . . . You know that. I can't even begin to tell you how much I . . . Danny, I . . . I . . . don't even know what to say. But, what about me? What about our baby?

(Danny doesn't respond. Betty takes his hand and puts it on her stomach. He pulls it away.)

DANNY: You know I can't leave Sarah . . . not now . . . It's still too soon. I won't do that to her. You don't know what she's going through. You have no idea—or even how I feel!

BETTY: I do understand. And I'm grieving for you, too.

DANNY: We need time. You've got give us that!

BETTY: Give you time? That's fine. But I'm not staying in this house with him any longer. I can't. Don't expect me to stay here until you're finished grieving—because you're never going to finish grieving. It's impossible and that I do understand. All I can say is that I'm sorry, but you have to know that things are different for me now. I'm carrying our baby, and babies don't wait. I don't know where I'm going, but I'm not going to be HERE when he returns Saturday. *(Betty goes to the closet, gets out a suitcase, and starts to pack.)*

DANNY: *(Pleading.)* Please, please . . . just wait. Let's not spoil what we've been given today. Please. I . . . I . . . just need a little more time . . . I promise. You and the baby . . . you're the most important things in the world to me. Come on. I didn't mean what I said. I'm sorry. Now come back over here. I don't want you upset.

(Betty walks over and sits down next to Danny. He puts his hand on her stomach and speaks to it.)

DANNY: Hi, Ally. She moved! She moved again! Did you feel that? She moved!

(They both laugh. They kiss.)

DANNY: Come on. I'll help you pack. I want you and the baby out of here. I'll find us a little place for the time being. I'll tell Sarah when I can.

BETTY: Oh, thank you. I love you so much.

(They start to pack.)

AMANDA AND JOE

(1 male/1 female, comedy)

BREAKDOWN Amanda and Joe are neighbors. They have never met. Joe
is a heroin addict.

SETTING The living room of Joe's small, single apartment.

• • •

*(Joe—on his knees, with his back to the audience—with urgency,
rolls up one sleeve of his shirt, pulls his belt out of his jeans, wraps
it around his arm, takes a needle, and shoots up heroin, then removes
the belt. He collapses onto a pillow propped against a crate. After
a few seconds, there is a knock at Joe's door. The door is already
slightly ajar, and Amanda quickly and frantically enters, closing
the door behind her. She looks through the peephole. Then, without noticing Joe, she runs to the window and looks out, then turns
to Joe. Joe is slowly sliding the needle behind the pillow.)*

AMANDA: *(She gasps.)* I didn't see you. I'm sorry . . . your door
was open. I'm locked out. I live across the hall. I've lost my key,
and the batteries in my cell phone are dead. *(Amanda holds up
her cell phone, waving it at him.)* See . . . No batteries. I'll need
to use your phone. I promise I'll only be a minute . . . Are you
OK?

JOE: Ooooh . . . yeah, baby. I'm cool. So whaddya you say? How
can I be of service to you?

AMANDA: Uhhh . . . well . . . I need to use your phone. *(Amanda
holds up her phone again.)* No batteries. *(She holds up her purse.)*
No key. I think someone is following me . . . My ex has my
spare key. Would you mind if I use your phone? I might have
to stay a little while. He can be here in no time.

JOE: Nooo problemo. Just put a quarter in the cup when you're done.

(Amanda quickly walks to the phone and picks up the receiver. She looks around the room noticing there is no furniture—just a crate and a pillow.)

AMANDA: Did you just move in . . . or are you just moving out? *(Amanda jiggles the phone. There is no dial tone.)*

JOE: I'm here. I mean I live here. My things haven't arrived yet. Actually . . . I was robbed. The dude took everything I have.

(Amanda replaces the receiver.)

AMANDA: Oh, my God! While you were here? You were robbed while you were living in this apartment building? Our building has robbers? Oh, my God! I knew it. Someone WAS following me. *(Amanda runs quickly to the door and looks through the peephole and then crosses to the window and looks out.)*

JOE: It's OK. It happened in my last apartment. Yeah . . . I had a penthouse.

AMANDA: You mean, these are all the belongings you have left to your name?

JOE: Yeah. Heeey, it's OK. I'm one of those minimalists. You want to use my cell phone . . . go for it. It's around the corner in the bathroom in my jacket pocket. I have an appointment. I have to be somewhere, so . . .

(Amanda quickly goes into the bathroom, and there she discovers a python in Joe's bathtub. She screams and comes running out.)

JOE: Hey! Look! I've had just about enough of your drama for one evening. Now, I'm gonna call the police on you.

AMANDA: You don't seem to understand. There is a HUGE snake in your bathtub. I think it probably came up through the drain. I don't know. It's unbelievable. It's tail was . . . Oh, my God!

(Joe looks at her and laughs.)

AMANDA: You think that's funny? You are really sick, you know that? You are a sick man. I can't believe I live across the hall from such a sicko on top of everything else.

(Joe casually gets up and glides to the bathroom. From the bathroom we hear a loud groan, some bumping and thumping sounds, more groans and yelling, more thumping, and then silence. Amanda stands by horrified. She opens her purse, frantically searches through her belongings, pulls out a pill box, pops a pill in her mouth, and tries to calm herself.)

AMANDA: *(Calling out to Joe in the bathroom.)* I think we should call the cops or the A.S.P.C.A.

(Suddenly Joe pops out of the bathroom and begins to frantically hide his drug paraphernalia.)

JOE: *(Shaken.)* Hey, look, I don't want any trouble with any A.S.P people or any cops.

AMANDA: Don't worry. We have no phones. That thing ate your cell phone and your jacket.

JOE: Oh, that's just great! Let's clear out of here. Maybe we should just go get a latte or something.

AMANDA: *(Looking through the peephole.)* I don't think we should go out THERE.

JOE: Maybe you're right.

(Amanda goes to the window and looks out.)

AMANDA: If I could just stay a little while. It'll be light soon.

JOE: Look, just try to relax a little. You need to relax.

AMANDA: How can I relax with a prehistoric monster in your bathroom and two men following me? Did you wash your hands?

JOE: I thought you said one guy was following you.

AMANDA: I don't know. *(Amanda sits on the floor and frantically digs around in her purse for a cigarette.)*

JOE: You're a good-looking girl. What's your name?

AMANDA: *(Looking him over suspiciously.)* My name is . . . Marge. Yeah . . . my name is Marge. *(Amanda continues to dig frantically in her purse. She retrieves a cigarette and continues to dig for a match.)* Do you have a light?

JOE: Oh, now Marge . . . You shouldn't be smoking. It's not good for you.

AMANDA: Look . . . Oh, never mind.

JOE: What's your old man's name?

AMANDA: Who?

JOE: The dude who has your key. What's his name?

AMANDA: Oh . . . his name. *(She thinks for a second.)* Uhhh . . . Joe.

JOE: Joe! You're kidding. My name is Joe!

(A loud thudding noise comes from the bathroom. Amanda and Joe both scream and grab each other.)

JOE: Now calm down! You have got to calm down! You're going to upset Amanda again.

AMANDA: Amanda . . . who's Amanda?

JOE: My snake.

AMANDA: You mean that thing lives here?

(Amanda breaks loose from Joe, quickly crosses to the window and looks out, then back to the door and looks through the peephole.)

AMANDA: I think I'll just go now. Maybe I'll see you around. By the way, my Joe is a cop slash detective and is really experienced in that karate stuff. As a matter of fact, he's right now practicing to be a Navy Seal . . . while he's in jail. Yep . . . he's in jail. He'll be out today. He killed two people. He was there for killing two people . . . in cold blood. See ya. *(Amanda exits, backing out the door.)*

ARMADILLO

(2 males/2 females, comedy)

BREAKDOWN Two old friends, Marge and Sharon, meet at a bar. Marge has just been fired; Sharon is in her last month of pregnancy.

SETTING A popular, dimly lit bar in Manhattan.

• • •

(Sharon is sitting at a bar alone, sipping her drink. She looks at her watch, then puts on her coat and takes one last sip when Marge enters.)

MARGE: Hi. Thanks for meeting me. I hope I didn't keep you waiting too long. Wow, you look great! How do you feel?

SHARON: Really good. I walked all the way from 81st Street . . . It's OK, the doctor said walking was good for me. Now you . . . you sounded so upset. How are you? Are you going to be OK?

MARGE: No! Yeah. No! Actually, I hate him! I know I came across like a good sport after he fired me. But the truth is I hate his guts. I hope he . . . I hope he . . . I hope he loses all his money! No worse . . . I hope he loses all his poofy, puffy hair!

SHARON: *(Laughs.)* You came across great, and he shouldn't have fired you! You were the best project manager they had!

MARGE: I know, but I still can't believe it! What are you drinking? Bartender, straight Tequila, a shot—make it a double. What are you having?

SHARON: Tea. Doctor's orders . . . and no, I don't mind.

MARGE: I felt like such a fool—a total loser. You saw the other girls ganging up on me—especially that one bitch . . . I mean totally. ME, head of . . .

(The bartender hands her, her drink.)

MARGE: Oh, thanks. *(Marge takes her drink, does the salt, the lime, downs the Tequila, and continues to talk.)* What was I saying?

SHARON: Head of your class at Yale . . . a Rhodes Scholar . . . magnum cum laude . . . junior partner of the biggest law firm in New York, etc., etc.

(Marge waves to the bartender.)

MARGE: Another shot—make it a triple!

SHARON; Whoa, you gonna be OK?

MARGE: Don't forget—nobody can outdrink me either! God! I hate him! "Marge—you're fired!" I will hear those words forever. What a nightmare. I'll never be able to face . . . *(Marge notices Jim and Tad entering the bar.)* ON NO! OHHH NO! Look who's coming.

(Sharon looks.)

MARGE: Don't look! Oh, it's too late.

(Jim and Tad walk over to Marge and Sharon. The men are drunk.)

MARGE: *(Sweetly.)* Hiii!

JIM: Hey!

TAD: How are you doing?

MARGE: Great! Oh, meet my friend, Sharon.

SHARON: Hello.

(Both men zoom in on Sharon.)

JIM: Heey.

TAD: How's it going?

SHARON: I'm good, thank you.

JIM: *(To Marge.)* You're a class act! You did great!

MARGE: Thanks—you're prejudiced.

JIM: No, really, you were great. What are you drinking?

MARGE: Tequila—and I'll have just one more eensy-teensy-weensy shot. Bartender . . .

SHARON: Are you sure?

MARGE: Sure. I've got my car. You can be the designated driver. Bartender, another shot. *(Marge holds up three fingers.)*

JIM: Hey, let's celebrate. A round for us . . . and the pretty ladies. Doubles?

TAD: Triples! *(Tad stumbles and falls on the floor disappearing behind the barstools. They all laugh. Tad pulls himself up to a barstool.)* I'm cool . . . I'm cool . . . It's all good. I can handle it. A TOAST! . . . Screw Trump! And his towers!

JIM: HERE! HERE! To beauty and brains!

(Tad to Sharon.)

TAD: To . . . ?

SHARON: Sharon.

TAD: SHARON!

TAD: And that chick, Armadillo . . . what a cooold bitch . . .

MARGE: Esmeralda.

SHARON: Amarosa.

TAD: A TOAST! Here's to . . . Ama . . . Arma . . . .

SHARON: Amarosa.

TAD: AMAROSA! *(Tad falls down on the floor again, and they all laugh.)*

SHARON: *(Grimacing in pain.)* OOOOhhh.

(Tad struggles back up to his chair. Marge and Jim are singing.)

TAD: What was that?

JIM: I don't know.

SHARON: *(Louder.)* OOOOOHHHHH!

(They all look at Sharon and freeze.)

MARGE: OH NO!

SHARON: It's time!

JIM: Time for what?!

TAD: Another toast!

MARGE: NO! She's having a baby!

SHARON: OOOOOOOOHHHHHH! *(Breathing short breaths.)*

TAD: OH . . . UH . . . What are we suppose to do?

JIM: I don't know.

MARGE: Bartender, HELP! Call a taxi!

TAD: No! Call the fire department! I saw that on *E.R.* They always call the fire department. Here's to the FIRE DEPARTMENT!

JIM: HERE! HERE!

SHARON: OOOOHHHH!

MARGE: Honey, just hold on, relax! Hold my hand! BREATHE!

TAD: Somebody boil some water! Why do they always say that in the movies?

JIM: I don't know.

MARGE: Be serious!!

TAD: If it's a girl, don't name her Armadillo!

JIM: HERE! HERE!

(Jim and Tad laugh.)

MARGE: I said be serious! Breathe, honey, breathe! And if it's a boy, don't name him Donald.

BEST FRIENDS

(2 males/1 female, drama)

BREAKDOWN Sonny and Norma Jean have been best friends since child-hood. He is secretly in love with her.

SETTING A small town in Texas, in the garage at Sonny's house.

• • •

(Sonny is in his garage repairing an old ice-cream maker. There is a radio playing some Chris Isaak music in the background. Norma Jean, dressed provocatively and barefoot, tiptoes up behind Sonny and puts her hands over his eyes. She speaks with a sultry, long, drawn-out Texas accent.)

NORMA JEAN: Hi.

SONNY: Oh, hi. I didn't hear you come in.

NORMA JEAN: What are you doin' there?

SONNY: Oh, not much . . . just piddlin' around.

NORMA JEAN: Looks like a pretty old ice-cream maker.

SONNY: Yeah, but it's just about to get put back together.

NORMA JEAN: You sure are good at that kind of stuff. You wanna come over later . . . for some ice tea . . . or somethin'?

(There is a pause as Sonny looks her over.)

SONNY: Now, whaddya think you're up to? Huh? Where's Tony?

NORMA JEAN: Now, don't look at me like that. And I don't care where Tony is. Anyway, you know where he is. He's out with that slut. He don't care nothin' about me or the baby . . . Look,

I don't want to be by myself all night. You could come over for a little while, couldn't you? Please. He's gonna be out all night.

SONNY: No, I'm not gonna let you get yourself into hot water with him. He's crazy. I don't even know how you got hooked up with him.

NORMA JEAN: I just need you to hold me. I've been through a real hard time since Mama died. She was always there for me. I could talk to her.

SONNY: You're still a little girl, aren't you . . . missin' your mama. I don't blame you. She was a good woman. I miss her, too. I'm sorry you don't have her now . . . but she's in a . . .

NORMA JEAN: Please, come over tonight . . . just for a little while. I'm gonna be stuck there all night long all by myself with the baby. I just can't bear it.

(Sonny digs into his pocket and takes out a small gold ring with a ruby in it and looks at it.)

SONNY: I want you to have this.

NORMA JEAN: Why that's beautiful! How come you're giving it to me? Where'd you get it?

SONNY: It was my grandma Lucy's. I found it in one of her dresser drawers when we sold her house. I've carried it around with me ever since for good luck and to remind me of her. Here . . . you take it now.

NORMA JEAN: Oh, I just couldn't.

SONNY: Please . . . I bet it'll make you feel a lot better right now, even better than a hug.

NORMA JEAN: No, I just couldn't.

(Sonny takes her hand and slides the ring on her finger. Norma Jean puts her arms around Sonny and gives him a good hug. He hugs her back.)

SONNY: You sure are a pretty little thing, and you got a good heart. Why do you take that from Tony?

NORMA JEAN: He used to be nice.

(Suddenly a car drives up and screeches to a halt. Tony jumps out.)

TONY: What are you doing here? And you, punk, get your hands off my wife.

NORMA JEAN: Oh, Tony, just go away. We were just sittin' here and you know it.

TONY: Shut up, bitch!

SONNY: Hey, don't talk to her that way!

TONY: I said get away from my wife, punk.

SONNY: Look, nothin' was going on here. You're drunk. Now let her alone. She's having a hard time over her mother . . . in case you haven't noticed.

TONY: And what do you know about my wife?

NORMA JEAN: Tony, just shut up! Where's your slut? Huh? Just go back to your slut!

TONY: You're the only slut around here!

SONNY: Hey, now back off. You're drunk and I don't want to hurt you.

TONY: *(Laughing.)* Oh, a real tough guy. I'm reeeal scared.

SONNY: I'm warning you. You don't want any trouble from me.

(Tony grabs Norma Jean by the hair, pulls her over to him, takes out a knife, and holds it to her throat.)

TONY: Now you shut up or I'll slit her throat. And if I ever see you around her again, I'll cut your guts out. Now she's coming with me. I've got some business with her.

SONNY: OK . . . take it easy. Now, just calm down. You don't really want to hurt her. C'mon now, just let her go.

NORMA JEAN: Tony, let go of me! You're hurting me!

(Sonny goes to take the knife from Tony, and Tony shoves it into Sonny's stomach. Norma Jean screams. Sonny backs up. He has both his hands around the handle of the knife. He drops to his knees and falls forward. Tony runs to his car and takes off. Norma Jean drops to her knees and wraps her arms around Sonny.)

NORMA JEAN: Sonny! Sonny! Oh, my God, somebody help us! Please help us! Sonny, don't die, please. Sonny, don't die. I love you, Sonny. Please don't die.

CASTING CALL

(1 male/1 female, romance)

BREAKDOWN Debbie and Sean are auditioning for a television series that is being kept confidential. Sean has already been cast in the lead role. The studio is using a scene from *The Newlanders* to audition the actors.

SETTING A casting office at Paramount Pictures.

• • •

SEAN: I'm coming *meine Dame*. I'm coming!

DEBBIE: I demand to be returned to the ship. I will not get back on that godforsaken wagon! You have had more than enough time to find Gottleib's cousin, or whoever he is. You are more interested in selling those unfortunate people you have chained up like monkeys.

SEAN: *Meine Dame*, it is Sunday. I can do nothing today. All the bureaus are closed.

DEBBIE: They were not closed yesterday!

SEAN: *(Pleading.)* I am working as fast as I can. Please be patient.

DEBBIE: *(Demanding.)* Take me to the ship! I wish to be with my children. We will wait onboard for Gottlieg. The ship might have arrived already.

SEAN: *(Threatening.)* It is quite impossible, *meine Dame*. I must ask you to quiet down, or I shall have to take measures to see that you do.

(Debbie grabs Sean's shirt with her left hand while faking a hard slap with her right hand. Sean stumbles backward against the wall.)

CASTING PERSON: All right! That was excellent. Just excellent, Debbie. You're with Lawrence and Fuller Associates—right?

DEBBIE: Yes, Jay Davis.

CASTING PERSON: Thank you, Sean . . . excellent, as usual.

(Sean gives the casting person a little salute.)

SEAN: Thanks.

CASTING PERSON: Hang around for a minute. I would like to see if Ray Starkie is available to meet Debbie. Sean, if you have to, you can take off.

SEAN: That's OK. I can stay.

(The casting person exits the office. The actors sit down on a sofa together.)

SEAN: You were great! She hasn't asked any of the other actresses I've auditioned with to meet Ray.

DEBBIE: Really?

SEAN: Really. You're the only one who had the rage needed for this scene. And we were so connected. It felt great.

DEBBIE: Yeah, I felt it too. Well . . . I guess we'll just wait and see. It's interesting that they're keeping the script such a big secret. I didn't even get a breakdown. Did they tell you anything?

SEAN: I can't say.

DEBBIE: Oh . . . OK.

SEAN: Where are you going from here?

DEBBIE: I was going to go workout . . . but I feel like I just had my workout.

SEAN: Want to have some dinner with me? We'll go healthy . . . since I'd be taking you away from your workout.

DEBBIE: Ohh . . .

SEAN: Ahh . . . you . . . I'm sorry. I should have asked . . . Are you uh . . . do you . . .

DEBBIE: Have a guy? Not at the moment. And I would love to have dinner with you.

SEAN: OK. You pick the place. What's your favorite food?

DEBBIE: Ummm . . . let's see . . . I like everything. We could go across the street to Lucy's Adobe.

SEAN: I had lunch there. *(They laugh.)* Let me surprise you.

DEBBIE: OK. Should I go home and change?

SEAN: No . . . I'll cook for you at my place. We'll celebrate.

DEBBIE: Celebrate?

SEAN: Yeah, we're going to be working together, aren't we? Besides I'm writing a play, and I'd love to have your opinion.

DEBBIE: Uh-huh.

SEAN: *(Seriously.)* No, it's not a line. I would really love for you to read it. I saw your reel yesterday, and I was just blown away by your work. I'm a big fan.

DEBBIE: I am really flattered.

SEAN: I have a feeling we're going to know each other for a long time. Now, I'm really getting ahead of myself. I've just blown my cool.

DEBBIE: That's impossible!

(The casting person peeks her head in.)

CASTING PERSON: Ray's on the phone now. It will be a couple more minutes.

(The casting person closes the door, leaving the couple alone again.)

SEAN: I guess you have your car here?

DEBBIE: Yeah.

SEAN: You can follow me.

DEBBIE: Where do you live?

SEAN: Right off of Mulholland Drive.

DEBBIE: Me too. I'm at Mulholland and Laurel Canyon.

SEAN: That's perfect. Let's stop at your house and leave your car. I don't want you out driving alone later tonight.

(The door opens, and the casting person enters with Ray.)

FAMILY SHOE STORE

(2 females/2 males, comedy)

BREAKDOWN Jackie and Hillary are best friends and are on a shopping
spree.

SETTING A shoe store in Dallas, Texas.

• • •

*(Two women enter the shoe store carrying shopping bags from
Barney's.)*

JACKIE: Good-bye Barney's.

HILLARY: Hello Family Shoe Store.

JACKIE: Hold me back if I try to buy more than three pairs.

HILLARY: OK.

*(Jackie moves quickly over to a table of handbags and starts to look
at them. Hillary runs over to a table of shoes.)*

HILLARY: Oh, look. These are gorgeous. Would you come here
and look. Aren't these great!

(Jackie runs over to Hillary.)

JACKIE: Uh-huh! To die for . . . oh, but look at these. I've been
searching for sandals this color all season.

HILLARY: Let's see. Yeah they're great . . . oh yeah these ARE great!
But you saw them first. You go ahead and try them on.

JACKIE: No . . . I don't care. You try them on, too. Really. I don't
care about that stuff. We'll just make sure we don't wear them
at the same time.

HILLARY: No . . . that's OK. Let's see how they look on you first.

JACKIE: Would you look at all the boots they have out already . . . and it's still July.

HILLARY: Yeah . . . and they'll be on sale by September, and who knows what will be stylish by winter. I wonder why they do that. It's ridiculous.

(Jackie picks up a boot.)

JACKIE: I might try this pair on. I really needed brown boots last year.

HILLARY: Actually, I did too. They're really good ones, aren't they. Go ahead, though . . . you saw them first. You try them on.

(The salesman enters as Jackie is trying to stuff her foot in the sample size 6 boot.)

SALESMAN: I'll be right with you.

JACKIE: OK. No hurry.

HILLARY: Well, I'm kinda in a hurry. I've got to get back to work myself.

(The salesman exits to the stockroom.)

JACKIE: Work?

HILLARY: Well, it's not like this place is overrun with customers. We're the only ones here. What's he doing back there?

(Jackie is still struggling to get the boot on.)

JACKIE: He's probably watching the news. There was a police chase going on all morning in Collyville. There was a woman driving this time. They got a little robot out there to see if there was a bomb in her car! I never watch that stuff.

(The salesman enters from the stockroom.)

SALESMAN: OK, now. I'm sorry I kept you waiting. How can I help you pretty ladies?

JACKIE: Are these on sale? *(Indicates the boot hanging off her leg.)*

SALESMAN: Yep. 40 percent off . . . Wait a minute . . . I'm not sure. Let me take a look. I'll be right back.

(The salesman exits to the stockroom.)

HILLARY: You'd think he'd know what's going on with his stock. *(Yelling to the salesman.)* Is the chase still going on?

JACKIE: It looks like it says they're on sale. Yeah . . . look. *(Pointing to a price tag that's on the bottom of the boot.)*

(The salesman peeks his head out from the stockroom. Jackie holds up a pair of sandals.)

JACKIE: Can I try these on, too?

SALESMAN: What size?

JACKIE: Ooh . . . a nine . . . nine and a half . . . ten . . .

SALESMAN: Sure, and how about the boots?

JACKIE: Yeah, the boots, too.

(The salesman looks at Hillary.)

HILLARY: I'll just look around a little more.

SALESMAN: OK, I'll be right back.

(Jackie struggles and finally gets the boot off. Hillary is looking around the store. The salesman returns carrying two boxes.)

SALESMAN: I only have size eights.

HILLARY: Oh! That's my size. I'll try them on.

JACKIE: Do you have two pairs of each? That could work for me, too. My feet vary in size.

(Hillary and the salesman glance at each other. Suddenly a robber enters with a stocking over his head carrying a large plastic orange soda bottle. He tries to crack it over a chair, but it doesn't break, so he throws the bottle down and grabs a high-heeled shoe.)

ROBBER: This is a robbery. Don't anybody move!

(He grabs Hillary and puts the shoe to her throat hostage style. He looks at Jackie.)

ROBBER: OK, bitch. Hit the floor!

(The salesman dives to the floor.)

ROBBER: I meant her, you idiot.

(Jackie runs and hides behind a chair.)

ROBBER: OK, punk, get up off the floor. Where's the cash register?

SALESMAN: It's locked. I can't open it unless I'm making a sale.

ROBBER: OK, I'll take three pairs of stockings! Now get up and get over to the cash register, you little punk, and make a sale. Now! Move!

HILLARY: Make the sale fast! My God—he's gonna kill me. Please I'm begging you. Oh, God, I don't want to die!

ROBBER: Shut up, bitch!

SALESMAN: *(Pleading.)* Please, I didn't say anything.

ROBBER: Not you, idiot. Now get over there . . . move . . . or somebody's gonna get hurt.

(The salesman scuffles over to the register.)

SALESMAN: Look, it's only ten o'clock. We've only been open an hour. There's not gonna be much money in the register.

ROBBER: Shut up man! Just shut up! Give me everything you've got . . . NOW! *(The robber struggles over to the register with his hostage.)* OK, now hand over the stockings . . . three pairs!

SALESMAN: What size?

ROBBER: Large.

(The salesman shuffles through the stockings.)

SALESMAN: We only have mediums. But they run large.

ROBBER: OK, I'll take those.

SALESMAN: Navy, white, black, or suntan? I think it's always a good idea to have an extra pair of navy.

ROBBER: No. Suntan will be fine.

SALESMAN: OK, that will be five ninety-five . . . plus . . .

HILLARY: IN THE NAME OF HEAVEN, MAKE THE SALE!

(The robber grabs three pairs of stockings and stuffs them in his jacket.)

ROBBER: Now, where's the safe in this place?!

SALESMAN: *(Pleading.)* It's in the stockroom. It's not gonna do you any good. I don't know the combination. I'm just a salesman. The owner doesn't give out the combination to the help!

ROBBER: Well, you'd better try to crack that safe or she's a dead lady!

JACKIE: Let her go!

ROBBER: Get down, bitch!

(The salesman dives to the floor again.)

ROBBER: Not you, you idiot! Now get the safe open before I kill them both!

HILLARY: Please, please do what he says. I'm begging you please.

SALESMAN: *(The salesman is still on his knees, groveling.)* I don't know the combination. I'm sorry. I swear. Please I swear . . . I don't know the combination . . . I swear really . . . I swear . . . All I want to do is sell shoes!

ROBBER: OK. OK. That's it.

(Jackie sneaks up behind the robber and hits him on the head with a boot. This does not even phase him. He slowly turns and just looks at her.)

JACKIE: Oh, my God!

(Hillary snaps her heel between the robber's legs. The robber screams, bends over in pain, and falls to the floor.)

JACKIE: C'mon let's get out of here. *(They all run out.)*

FEAR OF FLYING

(1 male/1 female, comedy)

BREAKDOWN Walter and Nina are strangers assigned seats next to each other on an airplane. Nina is afraid of flying.
SETTING On an airplane.

• • •

(Walter is a screenwriter sitting in the aisle seat of an airplane waiting for takeoff with his laptop computer in place. He is feverishly writing a horror film.)

NINA: Excuse me.

(Walter is startled by her voice. He looks up at Nina. His mouth falls open. She is his dream girl. She is a goddess.)

NINA: That's my seat.

WALTER: Ohhh . . . right . . . no problem. Let me, ahhh . . . move my stuff.

(Walter scrambles to pick up his scarf and coat from her seat and stuffs them under his chair. He then lifts his laptop over his head to let her pass. Nina slowly squeezes past him, stepping on his toes.)

NINA: Whoops, I'm sorry. *(Nina falls back into his lap.)* Whoopsy-daisy. I'm so sorry.

(The two struggle for a minute, and then she falls into her own seat next to the window. She pushes her bag under the seat and arranges her clothes.)

NINA: I wonder if they have any blankets and pillows. I'm going to try to get some sleep.

WALTER: I'll get one for you. They're probably in the overhead.

NINA: That's OK. Please don't bother. I'll look.

(Nina gets up. Walter lifts his laptop over his head to let her pass. She slowly squeezes past him again. She finds a blanket and a pillow in the overhead.)

NINA: Sorry, again.

(He lifts his computer over his head once more and raises his knees to his chest, allowing her to squeeze by.)

NINA: I'm a little afraid of flying. I plan on sleeping.

(She covers herself with the blanket and snuggles in. Walter closes his computer, slides it under his seat, and stares directly into the camera.)

WALTER: *(To the camera.)* I feel like I'm in heaven, sitting next to an angel, and we're still on the ground.

(Nina makes a few sounds, and then turns toward Walter. Still sleeping, her head falls onto his shoulder.)

STEWARDESS: *(To Walter.)* Please fasten you wife's seatbelt. We're about to take off.

WALTER: Sure. *(Walter looks straight into the camera and smiles, quickly glances at Nina, then looks back at the camera.)* OK, maybe I should wake her up. *(He gently shakes Nina on the shoulder.)* I'm sorry to disturb you, but you need to fasten your seatbelt. We're about to take off.

(Startled, Nina looks out the window.)

NINA: You mean we're still on the ground?!

(Nina frantically fastens her safety belt. Embarrassed, she smiles at Walter, then covers herself again and snuggles in. Walter looks

at the camera and starts to speak. The plane hits a pothole as it taxis down the runway. Nina suddenly grabs Walter on the thigh.)

NINA: *(Her voice projecting through the cabin of the airplane.)* What was that!? I heard a funny sound in the wheels! Did you hear that?! It sounded like one of the wheels fell off!

WALTER: No. No. No. No. No. They always sound like that.

NINA: Oh. *(Nina's eyes glance to the window. She takes a blanket and holds it to the side of her face to block her peripheral view of the window.)* Would you mind closing the shade for me? I can't stand to watch the takeoff.

WALTER: *(Walter speaks to the camera.)* Why do I feel guilty? I'm only trying to help a damsel in distress. *(Walter stretches his arm around Nina's back—taking the long way to the window—and leaning very close to her, he closes the shade. To Nina.)* There's no more looking out.

NINA: I'm so sorry. It's not fun feeling like this. You are so very brave and comforting. Do you mind letting me hold onto you, just for the takeoff?

(Walter, smiling, looks at the camera and quickly back to Nina.)

WALTER: No. Not at all.

(Nina wraps her arm around his arm as the plane takes off.)

NINA: Please . . . just keep talking to me. Keep me distracted. What's your name?

WALTER: Walter.

NINA: Walter? Walter . . . keep talking.

WALTER: What's your name?

NINA: Nina.

WALTER: Nina, you have beautiful . . . eyes.

NINA: Keep going.

WALTER: Yes, beautiful eyes.

STEWARDESS: You may now remove your seatbelts and move around the cabin.

(Nina is relieved. Water is disappointed. They both straighten up and adjust themselves.)

NINA: You are so sweet . . . I'm a little embarrassed, but you make me feel so safe.

WALTER: It was easy. I only told you the truth. You do have the most beautiful eyes I've ever seen.

NINA: You don't have to . . .

WALTER: No, you do. Are you visiting San Francisco?

NINA: No, I live there. I was visiting my mother in LA. She hasn't been well. Do you live in LA?

WALTER: No, San Francisco . . . and I'm sorry about your mother.

NINA: Well, that is so sweet. Thank you. You live in San Francisco too, huh? *(Seductively.)* Well, maybe we'll look each other up some time and . . .

(The airplane hits an air pocket. Nina screams and grabs Walter's leg again. He puts his hand on her hand.)

NINA: What was that?!

WALTER: Nothing, really. You're OK.

(Nina settles down again.)

WALTER: We're going to be landing soon. Would you like to have dinner with me, Nina?

NINA: I would love it. Excuse me, I'm going to the ladies' room. I'm sorry I have to pass you again.

(Walter looks at the camera. Nina squeezes by.)

NINA: I'll be right back.

WALTER: *(To the camera.)* I think I'm in love.

45 ACP

(1 male/1 female, drama)

BREAKDOWN Sherry and Ben are married with a baby. After sneaking out of their apartment in the middle of the night, Ben returns to find Sherry waiting for him.

SETTING In Sherry's and Ben's living room. It's 4:20 AM.

• • •

(Sherry is pacing back and forth in the living room. Occasionally she goes to the window, looks out, checks her watch, and then continues pacing. Finally, she sits down in front of the fireplace and sips on a glass of wine. She picks up a half-opened book and starts to read, but unable to concentrate, she puts it down. There is the sound of a key opening the front door. Sherry checks her watch again. The front door slowly opens. Ben enters and is startled to see Sherry.)

BEN: You startled me. I thought you would still be sleeping.

SHERRY: Where have you been?

BEN: Uhhh . . . riding around.

SHERRY: In the middle of the night. You smell like liquor! You're drunk!

BEN: Calm down!

SHERRY: Don't tell me to calm down! You sneak out in the middle of the night while we're sleeping?! What's that on your shirt?

(Ben looks down at his shirt and squints to see what Sherry is referring to.)

BEN: *(To himself.)* Blood.

SHERRY: Blood? Blood! How did you get blood on your shirt? Are you hurt? Let me see.

BEN: No. And I said calm down before you wake the kids! Now calm down! I mean it!

SHERRY: Don't you threaten me! And like you care about the kids?! Screw you! Now, you tell me where you've been.

(Waving her off, Ben slumps down into a chair and puts his head in his hands.)

SHERRY: Don't you dare wave me off!

(Ben does not respond.)

SHERRY: You have nothing to say.

(Sherry walks over to a table and picks up a printed e-mail and hands it to Ben.)

SHERRY: Your e-mail, I printed it out for you. What's this all about? Huh? Is THIS where you've been?

(Ben takes the paper, looks at it, then drops it on the floor. Sherry picks it up and reads the email out loud.)

SHERRY: "Ben, I need you. I am desperate. If I don't see you tonight I will kill myself. I can't live without you any longer. Love, Julie."

(Ben starts to sob as Sherry watches in disbelief.)

SHERRY: Why are you so upset? What's the matter with you?

(Ben doesn't respond.)

SHERRY: Answer me . . . Why are you so upset! Who's Julie . . . Oh, my God!

(We hear a child call out from his bedroom. Ben quickly dries his eyes.)

TYLER: *(From his bedroom.)* Mommy, something woke me up.

SHERRY: It's OK, baby. Go back to sleep. It's OK.

TYLER: I don't want to go back to sleep. I heard something. Please, Mommy, come and stay with me.

SHERRY: *(Whispering.)* I think you'd better tell me what's going on. Who's Juuuleee?

BEN: I don't feel like talking about it right now. Let's talk about it tomorrow. *(To himself.)* She was a friend.

SHERRY: What?

BEN: She was a friend.

SHERRY: I'll be right back.

(Sherry exits to the baby's room, then quickly returns.)

SHERRY: A friend? That "can't live without you any longer"? How long has this been going on?

BEN: Could you just stop asking questions! Get off my back!

SHERRY: Don't you dare raise your voice to me!

BEN: Look at you! You're going to wake up Tyler again.

SHERRY: I don't give a damn! Who is she! Are you having an affair with her?

(Ben looks at her but doesn't answer.)

SHERRY: Well are you?

(Ben still doesn't answer. She picks up a pillow and throws it at him, just missing Ben as he ducks.)

SHERRY: Answer me! Are you having an affair with her?

BEN: No, not any more . . . she killed herself tonight. I WAS TOO LATE!

SHERRY: She killed herself! Oh, my God!

BEN: Yes! She killed herself. *(Ben holds up the piece of paper and shakes it in her face.)* Like I said, I didn't get there in time. Now, let's go to bed.

SHERRY: Let's go to bed?! Are you out of your mind?! You can sleep right now?! What kind of person are you?! I don't even know you! You're sick. You've got a family here, and you've screwed everything up. I hate you right now. I hate you! I hate you! I hate you! I hope you die!

(Sherry falls onto the sofa and starts to sob. Ben waves her off with his hand, then staggers over to the desk, opens the drawer, pulls out a gun, and studies it for a moment. He then looks at Sherry and staggers out the front door. We hear a gunshot.)

GEOFFREY'S

(1 male/1 female, comedic drama)

BREAKDOWN Kyle and Glenda are brother and sister sharing a beach house in Malibu.
SETTING The living room of the siblings' beach house.

• • •

(Kyle is on the telephone speaking to his girlfriend.)

KYLE: C'mon baby . . . You know I don't like to . . . Yeah, but bbaby . . . sure I trust you . . . but a few people saw you . . . C'mon now, don't . . . now talk to me . . .

(Glenda enters the apartment, takes her coat off, throws it on a chair, then flops down on the sofa.)

GLENDA: Oh, my God! I'm exhausted!

(Kyle motions for her to be quiet, turns his back to her, and continues his conversation. Glenda doesn't notice.)

GLENDA: That bastard has such an ego! Every time I come up with an idea, he lovvvves it. Then suddenly, it's his idea. And who gets the raise? Not me . . .

(Glenda removes her shoes and rubs her feet. Kyle slams down the phone.)

KYLE: That bitch! She lied to me again! Four people saw her last night at Geoffrey's with some guy. Four people—and she still lies about it? I mean she's still lying. I would even consider taking her back if she would just admit it . . .

(Glenda lies down on the sofa with her feet up.)

GLENDA: The guy has no conscience. No integrity. He's totally immoral—ruthless. It's unbelievable. He knows when he's standing there lying to Marcus, pretending each time that it's his idea, I'm right there in the room! The guy has no shame . . .

KYLE: I can't believe it! What a liar she is . . .

GLENDA: How dare he . . .

KYLE: It's just not right . . .

GLENDA: No, it's not fair at all . . .

KYLE: That bitch!

GLENDA: That slime bag. I hate him!

KYLE: I hate her!

GLENDA: I've had it. I'm going to go up there tomorrow and give my notice. Do you agree? Don't you think I should do that? No more picking my brain. What do you think?

KYLE: I'm starving.

GLENDA: Me too. Do you want to go get something to eat? So what should I do? Tell me? Should I quit?

KYLE: No! I think you should write Marcus a letter and tell him what's going on. It's always better to put it in writing. Just tell him you're . . .

GLENDA: I mean I'm the one who's kept that company going. I've never even gotten a bonus. I'm really hurt. Why don't we go to the Real Inn and get some seafood.

KYLE: I thought we could go to Geoffrey's.

GLENDA: Oohhh, you just want to spy on Maria.

KYLE: Yeahh!! You're damn right!

GLENDA: OK . . . I'll pretend I'm your date. I'll go put on something really sexy, and if she's there, I'll throw myself all over you.

KYLE: Ohhh would you? Yeah . . . that'll show her!

GLENDA: Help me with the letter later?

KYLE: No problem. Go get changed.

(The phone rings.)

KYLE: *(A loud whisper.)* You get it in case it's her. Pretend you're my girlfriend. Go ahead—quick—before she hangs up.

GLENDA: *(With a Marilyn-esq breathy voice.)* Hello . . . Oh, that feels so good, Kyle *(Laughing.)* Ooohhh stop it . . . oh, wow. *(In her regular voice.)* Hello? Oh, hi Dad. No it's just me and Kyle. We were trying to make his girlfriend jealous. Did it sound like me? What's wrong? You sound funny. Is everything OK? . . . Oh, no!

KYLE: What is it?

GLENDA: *(Still on phone.)* Well, where is she?

KYLE: Who?

GLENDA: *(Still on the phone.)* Cedars. *(To Kyle.)* Get me a pencil. When did this happen?

KYLE: What is it?!

GLENDA: It's Grandma Mimi. She's . . .

KYLE: What? *(He grabs the phone.)* Dad, what's wrong with Mimi? . . . Well, can we see her? . . . What about tomorrow? . . . Well, what if something happens tonight? I won't ever get to see her again . . . OK. Dad, are you going to be OK? . . . How's Mom?

(Glenda grabs the phone.)

GLENDA: Where's Mom? . . . Well, I think we should go to the hospital tonight. She's going to need us . . . OK . . . we'll wait to hear from you tomorrow . . . *(Glenda hangs up. Pause.)* I can't believe this. I think someone should be with Mom. She's sleeping in the hospital room. What if Mimi dies and she's alone with her? Oh, Kyle, I don't want Mimi to die.

KYLE: She won't die. She's tough. *(Kyle wipes away his tears as he puts his coat on.)*

GLENDA: Where are you going?

KYLE: To get something to eat.

GLENDA: You better stay here just in case. Just order some pizza.

I SAW MOMMY KISSING SANTA CLAUS

(1 male/1 female, comedy)

BREAKDOWN Thelma, Jack, and their little boy Donnie have just returned from the mall where they saw Santa Claus.

SETTING In Thelma and Jack's living room, Christmas eve.

• • •

(Thelma enters the living room from Donnie's bedroom.)

THELMA: *(A loud whisper.)* I can't believe this! How could you have told him that?! You've ruined everything for him.

JACK: He could tell the guy wasn't the real deal. He saw the pillow, and the beard looked totally fake, and with some kind of accent—French or something. I don't know . . .

THELMA: You could have said his undershirt had pillow ticking . . . something, anything. And I didn't notice an accent. Why did you tell him there was no Santa Claus!?

JACK: I told him the truth!

THELMA: That there's no Santa?! You're going to warp his mind. Can't you just lie for once? And of all things to tell him, that Santa is really YOU! Who am I supposed to be—MRS. SANTA?

JACK: Yes.

THELMA: *(Pouting.)* No! I'm not! Mrs. Santa lives in the North Pole with Santa and Rudolf and . . .

JACK: OK, calm down before you wake him up.

THELMA: *(A loud whisper.)* So if you're Santa, he's probably having a nightmare right this minute about growing pointy ears and turning into a little elf. I'm going to go in and check on him!

JACK: Look, it's no big deal. I . . . didn't believe in . . . Santa Claus.

THELMA: Shusshhh! It's the truth after the truth after the truth. Can't you just tell one little old lie?

JACK: OK, if that's what makes you happy. I'll become a liar. I'll just sit down with him and fill him with lies.

THELMA: Now you're being sarcastic. You could straighten out a few things with him.

JACK: Like what else?

THELMA: Like Uncle Willie.

JACK: Yeah?

THELMA: You told him he was gay.

JACK: So?

THELMA: Yeah, and at show-and-tell he was telling everyone about his "happy Willie"! And then there was your lecture about the birds and the bees.

JACK: Oh, puhhh-leeezze.

THELMA: Don't act like it's no big deal. He is definitely going to need therapy.

JACK: You're overreacting.

THELMA: Not when he refuses to wear his bee outfit in the Spring Flower-fest.

JACK: What did you tell him?

THELMA: *(Reverently.)* I told him we found him in a basket on the front porch.

JACK: In a basket on the front porch?! We found him in a basket on the front porch?! I can see it all now—years in therapy from abandonment issues!

(Thelma thinks about this. A pause.)

JACK: *(Reassuring her.)* I was just kidding. He'll be fine. OK. OK. I'll lie from now on. I promise. I'll be the biggest liar in the world. Now come over here.

THELMA: *(Pouting.)* No.

JACK: Come on.

THELMA: No.

JACK: Santa's watching.

THELMA: Well, OK . . . if you promise to set things straight with Donnie from now on.

JACK: OK, anything you say. Now come over here.

THELMA: What about Peter?

JACK: Come over here. Who's Peter?

THELMA: Peter Cottontail. Can we still have Peter Cottontail?

JACK: Sure. Now come here and sit in my lap. Tell Santa what you want for Christmas.

(Thelma reluctantly, and like a little girl, goes over and sits in Jack's lap.)

THELMA: And for Valentine's Day, can we still have Cupid?

JACK: Especially Cupid. *(Jack holds some mistletoe over Thelma's head.)* Kiss kiss . . . *(He points to his cheek. Thelma kisses Jack on the cheek.)*

DONNIE: *(From Donnie's bedroom.)* I saw Mommy kissing Santa Claus.

A KISS GOOD-BYE

(2 females, drama)

BREAKDOWN Linda, the mistress of a recently deceased man, and the man's wife, Olivia, meet by accident in the funeral parlor the morning of the funeral.

SETTING A funeral parlor in Van Nuys, California.

• • •

(Linda is standing over a coffin, giving her last good-byes to her lover.)

LINDA: Oh, my God. I will never see you again . . . I will miss you so much . . . You've taken my heart and soul with you. Your last breath was with mine; our lips touching as we kissed . . . I still taste you . . . Good-bye my love, my precious love. Good-bye.

(She touches her fingers to her lips, then presses them to his lips. Olivia appears in the doorway.)

OLIVIA: What are you doing here? How dare you show up here today!

LINDA: Oh, I'm sorry . . . I never dreamed anyone would be here this early. I wouldn't have come here . . . Please . . . if I thought . . .

OLIVIA: Get out! You . . . You murderer. You killed my children's father. Now get out of here before I call the police!

LINDA: No please. What do you think the police will do when they get here? I know you're upset. But don't you know, you're the only one he loved.

OLIVIA: How would you know?

LINDA: Charles told me.

OLIVIA: What do you mean? He spoke about me? You actually talked about me when you were together? How dare you! How dare you! I hate you! I hate you both! I hate you! I hate him! I wish he were dead!

(Olivia slams her hand on the coffin, which causes his body to move. Both women jump back screaming as they hold on to each other.)

LINDA: He moved!

OLIVIA: I almost had a heart attack. Are you sure he's dead?

(They both start to laugh.)

LINDA: Yes. I think so.

(They continue to laugh.)

OLIVIA: This isn't funny.

LINDA: I know . . . I'm sorry. Look . . .

(Both women, out of breath, recovering from their ordeal, turn and sit down side by side in separate chairs. Pause.)

OLIVIA: You know, with four little kids you can get very tired. Men never seem to understand that. And it seems I was always exhausted.

LINDA: I was envious of you. Sometimes all he wanted to do was talk about you and the children. He's wild about the twins . . . was . . . *(Pause.)* I guess I'll be going. Olivia, I am deeply sorry . . . deeply sorry . . . for you and the children.

OLIVIA: I heard what you were saying to him . . . just now.

LINDA: Oh, don't believe a word. I was just being self-centered . . . dramatic . . . I don't know . . . Believe me, it was you he loved. And you have his children. That's what counts.

OLIVIA: Yes, and he was wonderful with the children. They adored him. It's going to be hard. They're young . . . I don't know how they'll deal with this . . . especially the twins. *(A long pause.)* And by the way, he was an amazing lover. After we made love each time, he would say it was like the first time.

(They look at each other for a moment. Linda starts to leave.)

OLIVIA: Linda, would you call me sometime? Maybe we could have coffee or lunch or something. You know . . . sometime . . .

LINDA: Are you sure? I would like that very much. Thank you. *(Linda pauses for a moment, then leaves.)*

A LITTLE TABLE IN THE CORNER

(1 male/1 female, drama)

BREAKDOWN Frank and Viola are lovers. They separated a month ago. Frank is an alcoholic.

SETTING At a small intimate restaurant in Greenwich Village.

• • •

(Viola is sitting at a small table having her lunch and reading a book. Frank enters and takes a seat nearby at another small table. After a few seconds, Frank raises his glass of water to toast Viola.)

FRANK: Salute.

(Viola looks up at Frank, smiles, then continues to read her book. Frank gets up and walks to her table.)

FRANK: I've been watching you . . . *(Pause.)* I'm not a stalker or anything like that. You just happen to be the most beautiful woman I've ever seen in my life. *(Pause.)* This is not just a line. You are breathtaking. Anyway I had to come over here and tell you that. Really, I was hoping to get a little closer to you. *(Pause.)* Could I ask your name?

(Viola looks up at Frank and smiles. Pause.)

FRANK: I'm going to be dreaming about you for the rest of my life . . . I would like to attach a name to your face. Just tell me your name, and I promise I'll leave you alone after that.

VIOLA: *(Smiling.)* Viola.

FRANK: No. Really?

VIOLA: Yes, really it's Viola. I was named after my grandmother.

FRANK: All right "Viola." Well, Viola, I promised to leave you alone now. The sight of you will never leave my mind. *(He turns to go back to his table, then turns around.)* May I join you?

VIOLA: I don't think so . . . Frank, it won't work this time.

(Frank sits down at Viola's table.)

FRANK: I'm different now. I'm a changed man. I haven't had a drink in a month now. I promised you I would change, and I have.

VIOLA: Frank, I am sorry . . . I'm sorry, but it's over with us now.

FRANK: How can you say that? I know you love me. You said you'd love me no matter what. That's the way I love you . . . no matter what.

VIOLA: You'll love me no matter what? Frank, what do you mean? OK, if you love me no matter what, then you'll understand that I can't take it anymore and that I'm never coming back . . . ever.

FRANK: You know this is hell for me. Not having you means it's all going to be in vain.

VIOLA: All going to be in vain? Don't do this for me, Frank. You have to do this for . . .

FRANK: I know . . . I know . . . *(Pause.)* You'll see one day, when I'm clean long enough . . . you're going to like the person you see sitting here now . . . and you'll want me back again.

VIOLA: No, Frank.

FRANK: Why do you feel like we're doomed? Why do you have to be so cold? At least be my friend. I would do anything for you.

VIOLA: Frank, please . . . I don't want you to do anything for me . . . just . . .

FRANK: I have to keep hoping.

VIOLA: Well, whatever it takes. Look, Frank . . . someday you're going to find somebody else.

FRANK: No. Don't tell me that. I don't want anybody else. You're my princess. I want you.

VIOLA: *(Holding back her tears.)* I'm sorry.

FRANK: I made a mistake. Please, I'm sorry I hit you that night. I hate myself for that. I can't take that back. I would die for you, and you know that. Just stick by me a little longer. I promise you, you're going to like the new me . . . you'll see . . . I promise.

VIOLA: I don't want your promises, Frank.

FRANK: Ohhh . . . I can't live without you. Please, come back to me, if I have to I will drop to my knees right here in front of everybody.

(Frank drops to his knees and takes her hand. She pulls it back.)

VIOLA: You're making a scene. Now go. People are looking at us. Just go.

FRANK: Just like that?

VIOLA: Get up! People are looking.

(Frank stands up.)

FRANK: Do you miss me Viola?

VIOLA: No. *(She takes her purse and walks out of the restaurant.)*

MAKING UP

(1 male/1 female, drama)

BREAKDOWN Rebecca and Dan, ex-lovers, broke up about two months ago.

SETTING In Rebecca's apartment in Santa Monica.

• • •

(Rebecca is putting the last-minute touches on her makeup. She puffs up a couple of pillows on the sofa, and then lights a candle. There is a knock at the door. Rebecca starts for the door, stops, and quickly returns to the mirror for one last look, then turns on the CD player. There is another knock at the door. Rebecca opens the door, to reveal Dan standing in the hallway.)

REBECCA: *(Seductively.)* Well, hello.

DAN: What took you so long?

REBECCA: I was just . . . come in. You look great.

(Dan enters the room and looks around at the familiar surroundings.)

DAN: Place looks the same. *(Dan points to the CD player.)* Hey, my CD player.

REBECCA: Wanna sit down?

DAN: Do all the rules still hold?

REBECCA: Ooohhh, come on . . . don't be that way . . .

DAN: *(Seriously.)* No kidding. Can I put my feet on the coffee-table? I don't live here any longer, so I shouldn't have to have rules now, right?

REBECCA: Would you like something to drink?

(Rebecca doesn't wait for Dan to answer. She walks over to a table and pours two drinks.)

DAN: No thank you. I can't stay long.

(Rebecca hands Dan a drink. He takes it. She sits down next to him. She holds her drink up to make a toast.)

REBECCA: To us.

(Dan doesn't respond as he downs his drink. Rebecca continues.)

REBECCA: It's good to see you. Thanks for coming over . . . Are you hungry? *(Rebecca starts to get up.)*

DAN: Nope. I just ate.

(There's a pause. Rebecca sips her drink as Dan continues to assess the room.)

REBECCA: Are you doing OK?

DAN: Do you really care?

REBECCA: Of course I do . . . I . . .

DAN: Of course you do?

(A pause. Rebecca takes Dan's empty glass and goes quickly to refill it. She returns and hands Dan his drink.)

DAN: I think the lady is trying to take advantage of the lad.

REBECCA: *(Playfully.)* I hope so.

DAN: I'm not going to let you mess with my head any more, you know that.

REBECCA: I never meant to. I missed you terribly . . . Can I kiss you?

(Dan doesn't respond. Rebecca leans into Dan and kisses him lightly on his cheek. He lets her. She takes his hand and lifts it up to her lips and gently kisses it as she looks into his eyes. She slowly stands up and starts to dance to the music. Dan sips his drink, reluctantly watching her, while hiding his enjoyment.)

REBECCA: Dance with me.

(She bends over, takes his hand, and pulls him up to her. They dance together.)

REBECCA: I'm so sorry I hurt you.

(They stop dancing and look at each other. Rebecca continues.)

REBECCA: I mean it. I am so sorry.

(She starts to kiss him, and Dan pulls away.)

DAN: I don't need your pity.

REBECCA: This isn't pity. I love you.

DAN: I have to go now.

(He turns and starts toward the door.)

REBECCA: Please don't go yet . . . I want us back again . . . the way we were.

(Dan stops and turns to her).

DAN: It's too late.

REBECCA: Too late? Don't you love me any more? . . . Huh? . . . I know you do. Just say it.

(Dan doesn't respond.)

REBECCA: I said I'm sorry, and I mean it with all my heart. I needed some time, that's all. We were fighting all the time. Dan, please . . . please forgive me . . . please?

DAN: Do you really think all this is going to change everything? Lady, you have no idea what I've been through.

REBECCA: I do. I know . . . and believe me, I'm sorry. What do I have to do? Tell me! *(She drops to her knees, desperately pleading.)* Dan, please forgive me. I want you back, Dan. Please . . . I'll make it up to you . . . you'll see. It'll be like old times. Dan, just, just give me a chance. Please, OK, please . . . you'll see. I'll do anything. Oh, God . . . Dan, please, please, please . . . I never meant . . .

DAN: I'm sorry. I just can't jump to your every mood. *(Dan starts to leave again.)*

REBECCA: Would a baby make a difference?

(Dan is stunned. He stops and turns to look at her.)

REBECCA: I'm carrying our baby.

DAN: Our baby? How do you know it's OUR baby?

REBECCA: Because it is. I haven't been with anyone else since you. It's true. I just needed some time, that's all. Please you've gotta believe me.

DAN: What about Rick?

REBECCA: Rick? That was nothing. I swear nothing ever happened between Rick and me. We're just friends. I promise.

DAN: Does he know about this?

REBECCA: NO! Of course not! What difference does it make?

(A pause as they stare at each other.)

DAN: How will I ever know you really love me? *(Pause.)* I'll never know . . . will I?

REBECCA: You'll know. Dan, nothing has changed. You'll see.

(Dan turns, walks out, and closes the door behind him. Rebecca drops her head in her hands. After some time, the door opens. Dan is standing in the door way. He goes over, sits beside her on the floor, and caresses her.)

DAN: Shushhh, don't cry. C'mon now . . . no more tears. Hey, I love you. We're having a baby.

MARY AND JOSEPH

(1 male/1 female, comedy)

BREAKDOWN At the office where Joseph works, the guys have a secret
Christmas lottery. The winner receives a half hour with a lady of the
evening, and Joseph is the winner.

SETTING Joseph's apartment, that evening.

• • •

*(Joseph is at the mirror, working on his hair. He unbuttons the
top button of his shirt, then quickly buttons it back up. He runs
to the sofa and puffs up the pillows. There is a knock at the door.
Joseph runs back to the mirror and works fastidiously on a small
clump of hair at his hairline above his right eye. Another knock
at the door. He slowly swaggers to the door and opens it.)*

MARY: Hi, Joseph. I'm a little early. Sorry. But my last "John" was
a little eager . . . over anxious . . . you know. Anyway, I'm ahead
of schedule. You don't mind, do you?

JOSEPH: Oh, no . . . well . . . I was just straightening up. Could
you wait outside for a minute while I finish?

MARY: I could . . . but it's kinda cold. It's snowing now.

(Joseph peeks out the door.)

JOSEPH: Wow, you're right. It's snowing . . . hmmm . . .
OK . . . I'll just be a minute. I was just getting the place in
order.

MARY: Do you mind? Really. I'm sure everything is wonderful. I'm
not that particular, Joseph. I'm cold.

JOSEPH: Oh, I'm sorry. Forgive me. Come in. Come in.

(Mary enters. Joseph scurries to the sofa, picks up a pillow, puffs it again, sits down, and holds it close to his chest. Mary sits down close to him.)

MARY: Wow . . . it's really warm and cozy in here. And your tree's so pretty and with all the lights. I see you like a lot of flowers, too, huh?

JOSEPH: Oh, yes. They're poinsettias. You don't see the white ones that often. They're a little more unusual. I'm into horticulture. The tree is a real tree. It's a living Christmas tree. Would you like to see my orchids? I have a greenhouse.

MARY: Sure . . . whatever turns you on. I never heard that one before. *(To herself.)* That's a first.

(Mary stands and slowly takes off her coat. She is dressed very skimpily. Joseph's mouth drops open.)

JOSEPH: Ahhh . . . you might want to keep your coat on.

MARY: Oh? It's cold in the greenhouse, huh? Well, I'm sure we'll get it nice and warm quick enough, and just think . . . what all that steam will do for your orchids.

JOSEPH: Ahhh, no . . . it's the neighbors. They might object. Their window is right next to the greenhouse.

MARY: Oh . . . good thinking. Well, we could stay in here. *(Mary seductively drapes herself on his sofa.)* Could I have a drink? Maybe a little Christmas toddy?

JOSEPH: Oh, sure, ha. What was I thinking?

MARY: Are you nervous? You seem a little nervous.

JOSEPH: Oh, no. I do feel like a kid at Christmas.

MARY: That could work . . . so why don't you bring that toddy over here to your mama.

(Joseph looks around the room.)

JOSEPH: Ah, to who?

MARY: Mama. Me. Your mama. My real name is Mary, but you can call me Mama.

JOSEPH: Oh, OK, Mama.

MARY: That's better. Now you just come on over here to your mama.

JOSEPH: Ahhh, do you mind if I call you Mary. "Mama" . . . that's what I call my, ahhh, you know . . .

MARY: Your mother? Sure, whatever turns you on. Mary wants to please Joseph. Now come here.

JOSEPH: Joseph? . . . Mary? . . . I . . . I don't know . . .

MARY: What?

JOSEPH: You know, Mary . . . Joseph . . . that's kind of weird, you know, with the Christmas tree and all.

MARY: Look, you know, we're going to have to watch the clock. You only won a half hour's worth. How 'bout Joey. Can I call you Joey?

(Joseph vigorously nods his head yes.)

MARY: Now, Joey, come here and tell Mary your secrets. Come here now.

(Joseph walks over and sits next to her on the sofa.)

MARY: That's a good Joey. Now tell Mary your secret wish.

JOSEPH: Well, I've always wanted to be an airplane pilot.

MARY: Yes? . . . Oh, I get it. OK . . . *(Mary stands up.)* Coffee, tea, or milk?

JOSEPH: Huh . . . Oh, I have coffee. Would you like some? Regular or decaf? *(Joseph starts for the kitchen.)*

MARY: No! No. Just stay right here. Sit down. Let's try it again. OK. Coffee, tea, or me?

JOSEPH: Coffee.

MARY: This isn't working. Are you sure you're into this pilot thing?

JOSEPH: Maybe not . . . You know . . . Silly me, I forgot . . . pilot . . . airplane. Can you believe it? I'm late for the airport. I'm leaving town, and I'm going to be late getting to the airport. *(Joseph runs to the window and looks out.)* Especially with this snow. I'm sorry. You'd better go so I can pack . . .

MARY: You might as well forget it. All the airports are closed because of the snow. Look, you're just a little nervous. Maybe you should have a drink. OK, Joey? Now where's the bedroom? I'm gonna make you a drink, go into the bedroom, get reeeeal comfortable, and wait for you. OK?

JOSEPH: OK.

(Mary pours Joseph a drink, gives him a wink, and walks languidly to the bedroom.)

MARY: Jo-eeey.

(Joseph runs to the mirror, and again works on that little unruly clump of hair.)

MARY: Jooooo-eeeey? Joey!

(Joseph gives up on his hair and dashes to the bedroom.)

MEDEA

(1 male/1 female, romance)

BREAKDOWN Melina is an actress rehearsing a scene for an important screen test. Johnny, her boyfriend—a successful director—is directing her in the scene.

SETTING The living room of Johnny's house in the Hollywood Hills.

• • •

(Melina is writing a love note on a gift card. She retrieves a small gift-wrapped box from her tote, slides the note under the ribbon, and quickly returns it to her tote as Johnny enters. Johnny reclines on the couch, picks up the phone, and speaks to his assistant.)

JOHNNY: Annie, Seth Rollins should be here shortly. Just let him in. Thanks.

MELINA: Should we get started?

JOHNNY: OK.

(Melina stands and slowly drapes a shawl around her shoulders.)

JOHNNY: *(Softly.)* Take your time.

MELINA: *(Enraged.)* "Oh coward in every way—that is what I call you, with bitterness, reproach for your lack of manliness—it is not . . . "

JOHNNY: *(Softly.)* That's wonderful. OK, now . . . this time, less anger.

MELINA: You're right.

JOHNNY: Have the anger but don't show it—otherwise the relationship is not clear. In the next scene you have to show it.

MELINA: Of course, you're right.

JOHNNY: OK, now what's the relationship in this scene?

MELINA: He must believe that I am his friend.

JOHNNY: How do you feel about him?

MELINA: I hate him.

JOHNNY: You loathe him. You despise him . . . but he can't know that.

MELINA: No.

JOHNNY: Right. Now make the stakes high . . . life and death. Start again. OK? Now loathe him—don't show it.

MELINA: OK. "Oh coward in every way—that is what I call you, with bitterness, reproach for your lack of manliness."

(The phone rings.)

MELINA: Damn!

JOHNNY: I'm sorry. *(He looks at his watch.)* It's probably Seth. He's late again.

(Another ring.)

JOHNNY: Johnny here . . . Hey what's up? . . . Do you want me to send a car for you? . . . OK . . . OK . . . Call my assistant Annie. Do you have her number? . . . Right. She'll have a car sent for you . . . Yeah, we're working . . . OK, call her. Get on it pronto . . . I understand. That's cool.

(Johnny hangs up the phone.)

JOHNNY: Damn rain! Coast Highway is closed down. This will really put us back. I wanted to get in a rehearsal with Seth. Anyway, you are wonderful in this scene. Just save your voice for later. Would you like something to eat? You haven't eaten anything.

MELINA: Sure.

JOHNNY: I'll have Annie call Orso for some lunch. Come here.

(Melina goes over and sits next to Johnny on the sofa.)

JOHNNY: What would you like to eat?

MELINA: Just some fruit and some hot tea.

(Johnny picks up the phone.)

JOHNNY: Annie, would you please call Orso and order some lunch? . . . About four people . . . Just salads, healthy stuff . . . You decide. Thank you.

MELINA: I would like to try it again once more from the top. I want to see if the relationship is clear.

JOHNNY: No, you've got it. You're brilliant. Save it for the test. Did you like seeing yourself in the scene yesterday?

MELINA: Actually, it was OK. I'm impressed. I really didn't think we could pull this off . . . you know . . . working together. You know you're my favorite director.

JOHNNY: It's an honor to direct you. Sal's going to be blown away by you in this piece. You're young for the role, but I wanted him to see your depth.

MELINA: Yeah, he's only seen me in sexy stuff. Hey mister, I love you.

JOHNNY: I love you, too.

(Melina reaches into her tote and retrieves the present.)

MELINA: Happy anniversary.

(Melina kisses Johnny on the cheek.)

JOHNNY: Don't think I forgot. One year today. I have a surprise. I'll be right back.

(Johnny leaves. The phone rings; Melina answers.)

MELINA: Hello. Ohhh no. Well are you OK? . . . I'm sorry. It's OK. We'll just do this when you can get out of there . . . I'll let him know. Just know your lines. Ha, ha. OK. We'll see you tomorrow. Bye.

(Melina yells to Johnny who is in the next room.)

MELINA: No more rehearsals. Seth said the road's gonna be closed all night. Let's go through my monologue one more time . . . pleeease . . .

(Johnny enters hiding something behind his back.)

JOHNNY: No, you've got it. Trust me. We're celebrating the rest of the day. Here, open your present.

MY LOVER

(1 male/1 female, comedy)

BREAKDOWN Aldo Bellalaqua is a famous and brilliant motion picture
director (any age from Tarrentino-esq to Scorsese-esq).

SETTING In a massive Baroque office at 20th Century Fox Studios.

• • •

*(Aldo is sitting behind his desk getting a manicure. The manicurist
finishes the last-minute touches and gathers up her things. Aldo
pulls out a $100 bill, gives it to her, and slaps her on the buttocks.
She giggles. They give each other a peck on each cheek, and she
leaves. Trying not to muss his nails, he carefully pushes the inter-
com button, buzzing his secretary.)*

ALDO: Maria, have any of the actresses arrived? *Buono* . . . Send
her in. By the way . . . if Sophia calls, put her right through to
me. *Grazie. Ciao.*

*(An actress knocks, opens the door and closes it behind her, then
leans against it, striking an elegant pose.)*

KAREN: Hello, I'm Karen Grey.

ALDO: *Ciao bella.* Come in. Sit down.

(Karen glides across the room and gracefully sits in a chair.)

ALDO: You are quite beautiful. *Bellisima!* Can you act?

KAREN: Yes, sir. I hope you'll be pleased.

ALDO: Do you have any questions about the monologue, Sharon?

KAREN: Karen.

ALDO: Who?

KAREN: Karen. My name is Karen.

ALDO: Karen. Well, you'll have to speak up. Don't be shy. You're an actress. Now are you ready?

KAREN: Yes, sir. *(Karen stands, clears her throat, and drops her head for a moment to prepare.)*

ALDO: What was that?

KAREN: What?

ALDO: Clearing your throat, bowing your head—What was that?

KAREN: *(Reverently.)* I was preparing.

ALDO: An actress prepares offstage!

KAREN: Yes, sir.

ALDO: Start again.

KAREN: *(Softly, with deep emotion.)* My lover . . . my beautiful lover . . . please, I beg you, don't leave me now . . . please. I need you so. We still have so much to do, so much to . . .

ALDO: Plead!

KAREN: Plead? OK . . .

ALDO: Aiyyy . . . don't stop. Just continue when I give you direction! Don't disconnect! Do you understand?

KAREN: Yes.

ALDO: Again. Now plead.

(Aldo mouths the words as she is acting.)

KAREN: *(Pleading.)* My lover . . . my beautiful lover . . . please I beg you, please, don't leave me now . . . pleeeze. I need you so. We . . .

ALDO: PLEAD!!

KAREN: PLEEEEZE I need you so. We still have so much to do . . . so much to give each other. I can't live without you my love . . .

ALDO: Louder!

KAREN: *(Angrily.)* I CAN'T LIVE WITHOUT YOU MY LOVE!

ALDO: Where did that anger come from?

KAREN: I'm sorry.

ALDO: You're sorry? Why sorry?

KAREN: I mean I'm sorry I got angry.

ALDO: No—you should be angry.

KAREN: I should?

ALDO: *(With deep emotion.)* Si . . . your lover is dying. You should be enraged. He is abandoning you.

KAREN: Oh . . . true.

ALDO: Of course. Now start again, and this time I want the truth!

KAREN: The truth! Yes . . . Still pleading? Angrily pleading?

ALDO: Si, Sharon!

KAREN: Karen!

ALDO: Karen! Si, si . . . with rage and pain . . . deep rage and pain . . . now start again!

KAREN: *(Pleading.)* Oh, my lover . . .

ALDO: *(Matter-of-fact.)* Don't add "oh."

KAREN: Sorry.

ALDO: I wrote the screenplay. The words are beautiful. Don't change them. Now start again.

KAREN: *(Desperately pleading.)* My lover . . . my beautiful lover . . .

ALDO: On your knees . . .

(Karen drops to her knees.)

KAREN: *(Groveling)* Please, I beg you. Don't leave me now. I need you so . . .

ALDO: Louder.

KAREN: Pleeeease . . . I need you so. We still have so much to do . . .

(The phone rings.)

ALDO: Pronto. Ahhh . . . mi bella Sophia! *(He puts his hand over the mouthpiece and speaks to Karen.)* Continue—anger, rage— and don't stop. Give me power! *(He continues his telephone conversation.)* Sophia, bella . . . ha . . . ha . . .

(Karen is still on her knees.)

KAREN: *(Groveling.)* My lover . . . my beautiful lover . . . please, don't leave me now . . .

ALDO: *(To Karen, covering the mouthpiece.)* Brilliant! Continue.

KAREN: My lover . . .

ALDO: Never mind. That will do. I will be in touch with you. *Grazie. Ciao.*

(Karen stands in front of his desk.)

KAREN: *(Deeply grateful.)* Thank you, Mr. Bellalaqua. It was a great pleasure to meet you. Would you like my picture and résumé or should I leave it with your secretary?

ALDO: Leave it on my desk, Sharon.

KAREN: Karen.

ALDO: Karen! *Grazie. Ciao.*

(Karen curtseys and leaves.)

NADINE'S DINER

(1 male/1 female, romance)

BREAKDOWN Nadine and Howard were lovers and broke up some time ago.

SETTING Inside Nadine's Diner in Dallas, Texas, at closing.

• • •

(Nadine starts toward the front door of her diner to lock up for the evening. There is a knock at the door.)

NADINE: *(Through the window of the front door Nadine speaks.)* Sorry, we're closed now. The cook's cleaning up.

HOWARD: I just want a quick cup of coffee.

(Nadine squints, presses her face to the window to make out the person outside. She opens the door.)

NADINE: Land's sakes! You old bulldog! When did you get into town? Get in here and get out of the cold!

(They give each other a big bear hug, and then look each other over.)

HOWARD: Let me see you. Yep, you still look like a movie star.

(Nadine whirls around to show off her figure.)

NADINE: I try. You still look like an old bulldog except no black eye.

HOWARD: Yeah, you got a good left hook.

NADINE: *(To the kitchen.)* Tootsie, I need a couple cups of coffee. Thanks, honey. Come in. Sit down. *(They both sit.)* I'm just speechless! So . . . How are you? What's up? You look good! I heard Sudie ran off with one of your hands. She tricked you into marrying her, huh? There was no kid after all. Well, you got what you deserved!

HOWARD: Do you feel better now? You still holding a grudge?

NADINE: You bet! If I weren't so glad to see you, I'd give you another black eye. *(To the kitchen.)* Hey Tootsie, how 'bout that coffee.

TOOTSIE: I'm makin' up some fresh. Hold your horses.

HOWARD: I heard you married Buck Willis.

NADINE: How'd that get all the way to Oklahoma? What else did you hear?

HOWARD: He's in the pokey doing time. Too many brawls . . . all caught up with him.

NADINE: That's right. That's right. I never see him. We're divorced now. He's as mean as a rattlesnake. Always up to no good.

(Tootsie enters with two cups of coffee.)

NADINE: Tootsie, this is Howard Farmer. Howard, this is Tootsie Williams.

(Howard rises.)

HOWARD: It's a pleasure, ma'am.

TOOTSIE: Enjoy the coffee. I'm gonna go finish up in the kitchen.

(They both drink their coffee.)

HOWARD: Mmm-mmm . . . good coffee.

NADINE: So, you haven't said what you're doin' back in Dallas. How long you been here?

HOWARD: Oh, a couple weeks.

NADINE: A couple weeks. Well, I'll be . . . You've been here a couple weeks and you're just now seeing me. Well, I'm hurt. I'm real hurt.

HOWARD: Now don't be. I needed to get myself settled in.

NADINE: Settled in? You mean permanent?

HOWARD: Uh-huh.

NADINE: What about your cattle ranch in Oklahoma? I heard you were doing great.

HOWARD: I was for a while, but the drought wiped me out. Just about everybody in Oklahoma got wiped out.

NADINE: Well, my Lord, Howard . . . I am so sorry to hear that. *(There's a pause, and she continues.)* Hey. I'll bet you could eat something. I'll have Tootsie make us up some eggs before she leaves. How's that? I didn't have time to eat anything tonight myself. Well, I'm just speechless! How'd you find me?

HOWARD: It wasn't hard. Nadine's is on the map. I see you're doing great.

NADINE: Yeah, I guess you could say that.

(A pause.)

HOWARD: I don't know if I ever said it . . . but I'm sorry about how things turned out between us. Real sorry. You didn't deserve . . .

NADINE: You said it, and I'm over it now. *(A pause.)* Hold on. I'll be back in a jiffy. *(After a few seconds, she returns.)* Tootsie's making us some supper. And then she'll be gone. I am just speechless! Sit back, put your feet up, and tell me your plans.

HOWARD: Well, I managed to hold on to enough money to get me a nice piece of land right outside of Dallas in Ennis, and I'm opening up a hardware store.

NADINE: Oh, I remember, you have a lot of kinfolk over in Ennis.

HOWARD: Yeah . . . and I'd be obliged to have you as part of my plans.

(A pause.)

NADINE: Really? Just like that?

(He takes her hand, and gently kisses it.)

HOWARD: Just like that. You're the prettiest girl in Texas. And I've never stopped thinking about you.

(Tootsie enters; Howard and Nadine quickly adjust themselves.)

TOOTSIE: Good night y'all. Have a nice supper.

THE OAK BAR

(1 male/1 female, romance)

BREAKDOWN Jan and Barry are ex-lovers. Each has married. They accidentally meet at a bar.

SETTING The Plaza Hotel in Manhattan at The Oak Bar, late afternoon.

• • •

(Jan is sitting at the bar listening to messages on her cell phone. She closes the phone, places it in her bag, and motions for the bartender.)

JAN: *(To the bartender.)* Could I have a check please?

(Jan reaches in her purse for her wallet, as Barry walks up quietly behind her.)

BARRY: Boo!

JAN: Stop that! You scared me! I can't believe you did that. I hate you for that.

BARRY: *(Laughing.)* I'm sorry. May I join you?

JAN: *(Pouting.)* No. And you're not sorry!

BARRY: Please. I'm really sorry.

JAN: No. I'm . . .

BARRY: *(Seriously.)* Really, I'm sorry. I caught a glimpse of you from outside through the window. I couldn't resist. I just had to say hello . . . Hello.

JAN: Hello.

BARRY: May I join you for a minute? I would love to know what you've been up to. I haven't seen your film yet. Your reviews are awesome.

JAN: *(Embarrassed.)* Oh, I'm just . . . I think I just got lucky. *(She notices that he is holding a bouquet of flowers.)* Who are the flowers for?

(Barry sits down next to her.)

BARRY: Oh, my sister, Cheryl. She had a baby last night. I was on my way over to the hospital to see her . . . a boy . . . she named the little guy after me.

JAN: Oh, that's wonderful—a boy. How is she doing?

BARRY: She's doing great. She's in a hurry to go home. You know Cheryl . . . nature woman.

JAN: Yeah. That's so sweet. She named the baby after you.

(Pause.)

BARRY: I heard you're not with Chuck any more. You're divorced.

JAN: Whoa—that sure got around fast.

BARRY: Who are you waiting for? I know you're not hanging out here alone.

JAN: I was supposed to meet a girlfriend . . . husband problems . . . but she had to cancel.

(Pause.)

BARRY: You spoiled me, you know. I really didn't know how good I had it. No one else could ever measure up to you.

JAN: How's Cindy?

BARRY: I deserved that. She's doing pretty good. You know her drinking has ruined everything. She's in another rehab. We've agreed to divorce after she gets out this time.

JAN: Well, I've finished my drink so I guess I'll be going.

(Jan picks up the check. Barry takes it from her.)

BARRY: No—don't go now—please. Please, have another drink with me. I would really like to sit here and . . . just talk.

(Pause. Jan looks him over.)

JAN: OK. One more, and then I have to go.

BARRY: Bartender, another one for the lady. And I'll have the same. Thanks, my man.

(Pause.)

BARRY: Ummm . . . I'm having a hard time holding back all the things I'd like to say to you . . . I still love you. I mean it. I wanted you back so bad—and then suddenly you got married.

JAN: At least Chuck had the time to be there for me. Anyway, you hurt me. I guess with Chuck it was rebound.

(Barry leans over and kisses her gently on the cheek.)

BARRY: You still smell the same. You drive me crazy.

(Jan starts to get up.)

JAN: Look, I'm sorry.

BARRY: No. Stay. Look, I . . . I . . . I beg you to forgive me. I'll keep begging you forever if that's what it takes. I screwed up. I would spend the rest of my life—if I had to—proving to you that I could be different. Tell me one thing. Do you still love me at all?

JAN: I don't want to get hurt again.

BARRY: Just tell me . . . do you love me? Do you love me at all?

JAN: Yes, I still love you.

(The bartender hands them their drinks.)

BARRY: *(Hands money to the bartender.)* Thanks. Here keep it.

(There is a long pause as they both drink.)

BARRY: I never stop thinking about you. I mean it. Everyday . . . you're always in my thoughts. It crushed me when you got married. Let's finish our drinks. We'll walk outside, get a taxi, and see where it takes us.

JAN: No.

BARRY: Yes.

(Barry stands, takes Jan's coat from the back of the chair, and wraps it around her shoulders. He takes her hand, and they exit.)

THE PROPOSAL

(1 male/1 female, drama)

BREAKDOWN Brenda and Cal have been lovers for a year.
SETTING In Cal's beach house in the Hamptons, evening.

• • •

(Cal puts on some music. He retrieves an engagement ring from his pocket, admires it, and returns it to his pocket. He goes to the table, moving to the music, and lights some candles. There is a knock at the door. Cal rushes back to the kitchen, returns with two champagne glasses, and sets them on the table. He goes to the door and opens it, revealing Brenda standing in the doorway. Brenda enters.)

BRENDA: Wow! You look hot! Oh . . . you're having a party. What's the occasion? Is all this for us?

CAL: Yes. This is for us. We've been together a year now, and I wanted to make everything special tonight. Sit down. No, actually, just give me your things. I want you to dance with me.

BRENDA: Oh . . . you know I'm a terrible dancer. I'll step all over you.

CAL: No, c'mon dance with me. I've never noticed you to be anything but perfect. Now come here and dance with me.

(They start to dance.)

CAL: You look stunning tonight. I'm a lucky guy.

BRENDA: Oh, you're embarrassing me. See, I just stepped on your toe.

CAL: I don't care. You can do anything you want to me. You're a goddess and I love you. I love you. Do you hear me? I love you.

BRENDA: What happened? Did you win the lottery?

CAL: Yes . . . my divorce is final today.

BRENDA: Wow! Did you know this was about to happen? You never mentioned anything about it . . . only that it was in the works. That was kind of fast, huh?

CAL: Six months. It was an eternity. Anyway, I have connections. Sit down. I have something for you.

(Brenda sits down. Cal gets down on one knee and gently takes her hand and kisses it.)

CAL: I love you deeply with all my heart. You are the most beautiful and the most wonderful woman in the world. And I want to take care of you for the rest of my life . . . and grow old with you . . . Will you marry me?

(Cal takes the ring from his pocket and slides it on her finger.)

BRENDA: It's breathtaking!

CAL: It was my mother's wedding ring and before that my grandmother's. She wanted you to have it. You know she loves you, too.

BRENDA: It's gorgeous. I'm dumbfounded. I'm afraid I'll lose it.

CAL: You won't. If you do, so what. It's just a ring. It looks beautiful on you.

BRENDA: Cal . . . I can't accept this.

CAL: Sure you can. It would upset Mother terribly if you didn't wear it. You'll get your wedding ring from me later . . . before the wedding. We'll pick it out together.

BRENDA: *(Deeply sorry.)* Cal . . . I can't marry you.

(Brenda hands him the ring back. A pause.)

CAL: Why?!

(Brenda takes Cal's hand and looks deeply into his eyes)

BRENDA: *(Tenderly.)* Cal . . . you mean everything to me, and I've loved everything we've shared this past year, and I'll never forget a single moment. You'll always be special to me, Cal . . . and I'll always love you but . . . there's someone else.

CAL: Someone else? What do you mean? You've been cheating on me?

BRENDA: No! It just happened. I didn't mean for it to.

CAL: Who is he? Are you sleeping with him?

BRENDA: Cal, please.

CAL: Does he know about me?

BRENDA: No, not yet.

CAL: What's his name, huh? Give me his phone number. I'll just call him now and tell him what a slut you are.

BRENDA: Cal, stop it!

CAL: Who is he? I want to know something about my competition.

BRENDA: It doesn't matter.

CAL: It matters to me! I bet it'll matter to him too when he hears you're sleeping with someone else.

BRENDA: I'm sorry. I'm leaving now.

(Cal goes and locks the door and grabs Brenda's arm, pulling her to him.)

BRENDA: Cal, please. Let me go.

CAL: No. You're gonna be with me tonight. You're mine tonight. I'll pass you on to him when I'm done with you.

BRENDA: *(She starts to cry.)* You're scaring me. Please, Cal. Stop it. I swear, I didn't mean for this to happen. Let me go. You're hurting me.

(Cal lets go of her arm, slowly slides down the wall, and starts to cry.)

CAL: Just go! Get out! I don't want you any more.

BRENDA: I'm sorry.

CAL: Get out! I hate you now. You've been with somebody else. I don't even want you now. You're used goods. I don't even want you now. Just get out of here.

(He continues to sob. She leaves.)

SING SING

(1 male/1 female, drama)

BREAKDOWN Marco tried to kill a man who raped his sister, Corrine. He is currently serving time in Sing Sing prison in New York for attempted murder.

SETTING Visiting area of the prison. (Note: The scene is enhanced if the actors have mastered a New York or Italian dialect).

• • •

(Corrine is sitting behind a glass partition waiting for Marco. Marco slicks back his hair with his hand as he enters. He gives his sister a smile and a little wave and sits down in a chair on the other side of the partition. They each pick up a phone.)

MARCO: *(Disappointed.)* I missed you last week.

CORRINE: I know. Me too. But I couldn't get here.

MARCO: How's little Manny? Did he get my letter?

CORRINE: Yeah, he got your letter.

MARCO: You look OK.

CORRINE: Oh, I don't.

MARCO: You do. I wish you wouldn't look so good. Make sure you keep yourself covered up.

CORRINE: I do. Don't worry. You look good.

MARCO: Yeah, I'm working out. *(Pause.)* You look sad. Maybe you shouldn't come for a while.

CORRINE: No, I like to come. I need to see you, Marco.

MARCO: No, I don't think you should come for a while. When you leave this place . . . I don't know . . . it gets hard for me too.

CORRINE: Marco . . . Mama died. She past away last week. The doctor said she had some kind of stroke or something. I'm sorry, Marco.

(Pause.)

MARCO: *(He starts to cry.)* I guess it was all my fault . . . keeping her all upset all the time.

CORRINE: No, Marco, it wasn't your fault. Mama was getting old. She was tired. It was her time.

MARCO: I wish we could have said good-bye. I didn't get a chance to say good-bye . . . Mama and me. I knew something was up when you didn't come last week. I was worried about you and little Manny. How is he taking it?

CORRINE: He's doing OK. I told him she was in heaven with Pop.

(Pause.)

MARCO: Was it a nice funeral? Did all the family come?

CORRINE: It was snowing. A lot of the family couldn't get there. It was real nice though. I mailed you a newspaper clipping from the obituary section. It's nice. It mentions you're her only son, and a lot of nice things about Pop and me . . . and that she had a grandchild, Manny. It mentions Manny. He liked that. And no—it didn't mention you were here. You'll see. You'll get it soon. I mailed it to you.

MARCO: How are you handling it?

CORRINE: I'm going to miss her.

(Pause.)

MARCO: Tell me what happened. Where did it happen? Was she in a lot of pain?

CORRINE: It was OK . . . if you gotta go. She died in her sleep. She said she was a little tired and went upstairs to bed and that was it.

MARCO: Who found her?

CORRINE: Manny.

(Pause.)

MARCO: Ohhh . . . that's no good. How's he doing?

CORRINE: I told you. He's doing OK.

MARCO: I'm sorry, Corrine. *(He motions to a guard.)* I gotta think about this a little bit. Do me a favor. Don't come back next week.

CORRINE: Don't go yet.

MARCO: No . . . I gotta do some thinking. They got some kind of little chapel here. I'm gonna go over there.

CORRINE: Mama . . . she loved you. You were her favorite you know.

MARCO: Yeah, you think so?

CORRINE: Yeah. I love you too. I'll see you next week.

SISTERS

(1 male/1 female, drama)

BREAKDOWN Sam and Jessie are married. Jessie is concerned when Sam is late coming home from work.
SETTING In Jessie's and Sam's living room.

• • •

(Jessie is reading a book. She puts it down and starts to make a phone call when Sam enters.)

JESSIE: Oh, thank God. I was worried. *(Jessie starts over to him.)* I've tried to call you—I don't know how many times. Where have you been? *(Jessie starts to hug him.)*

SAM: At Sharon's.

JESSIE: *(Confused.)* Sharon's? My Sharon?

SAM: Yes.

JESSIE: You look so serious. Is something wrong? What's wrong? You're acting funny. Is she OK?

SAM: Yes.

JESSIE: Well, you're scaring me.

(A pause.)

SAM: *(Matter-of-fact.)* I'm going to get a few things and then I'm going to be leaving.

JESSIE: Leaving? What do you mean . . . leaving? What's going on?

SAM: I'm trying to tell you. I'm . . . leaving you . . . tonight.

JESSIE: I don't understand.

(A pause.)

SAM: Jessie, it's over between us.

JESSIE: Over between us? Just like that? . . . Oh, my God. This is about you and Sharon, isn't it?

SAM: Yes.

JESSIE: What about Larry?

SAM: Sharon's telling him tonight.

JESSIE: I don't believe this. This is insane. How long has this been going on?

(A pause.)

SAM: *(Deeply sorry.)* A few months.

JESSIE: A few months? And Sharon's telling Larry tonight. What a neat little plan. *(A pause.)* Well . . . what . . . are you in love? I could see her flirting with you. You really fell for it. What a dummy you are. She does that with everybody she sees. You know that. You make me laugh. Poor Larry—he's put up with it for years. You're supposed to be his best friend! Couldn't you control yourself?! My own SISTER!

SAM: Jessie . . . *(He starts to move toward her.)*

JESSIE: Don't you come near me! How dare you! This is not going to amount to anything. Don't you know that?! You're just another one of her victims—another conquest. She'll be leaving you.

SAM: Not true.

JESSIE: Oooh . . . She "loves" you. Ha, ha, ha. Sure. I've covered for her for years. She can't love anybody but herself!

SAM: Shush. Keep it down.

JESSIE: Don't you shush me! Don't you dare shush me! I don't give a damn who hears me.

SAM: Please, Jessie. Please . . . I'm sorry.

JESSIE: No! You're not sorry. If you cared you wouldn't have let this happen. You let her ruin everything. She won't stay with you. She's had hundreds of "boyfriends." You're just another little nothing for her. She's always got to prove herself. You know that!

SAM: Look . . . I'm going now. I'm sorry. *(He turns and starts to leave.)*

JESSIE: Did you just fall out of love with me? What did I do wrong?

SAM: Nothing. You're perfect. I don't know. I'm so sorry that I hurt you.

JESSIE: Then why? How can you be with me like we were last night . . . and leave me tonight? I thought things were great with us. *(Pause.)* I know I'm tired a lot, with the kids and all. Come here. Come over here and hold me. Just for a minute. You can't leave just like that. Come here . . . it's me, remember? Jessie. *(She lets her robe fall off of one shoulder. Sam walks over and sits next to her and puts his arm around her. She takes his hand and puts it on her face, then kisses the inside of his palm. She starts to kiss him. Sam pulls back.)* Don't leave me. Don't make me beg you.

SAM: I don't want you to beg me. You don't deserve this. I mean it—you don't deserve this. You're too good for me. I can't help myself. *(Sam stands up and starts to leave.)*

JESSIE: What about me? What am I supposed to do now? What about the kids?

(Sam doesn't respond.)

JESSIE: If you leave me now . . . if you walk out that door . . . I'll kill myself.

(Sam turns and starts to leave, and then turns and looks back at Jesse. They each freeze for a moment. Sam leaves.)

SIXTH SENSE

(1 male/1 female, drama)

BREAKDOWN Travis has been blind for five years caused by a progressively degenerative disorder. He and Nicky have been living together for six months with her four-year-old daughter, Natalie.

SETTING The kitchen of Travis's apartment.

• • •

(Travis is preparing a salad at the island in his kitchen, as Katie, his housekeeper, who cleans once a week, enters the kitchen.)

KATIE: Bye Travis, I'm leaving now. You have a good week.

TRAVIS: You too, Katie. And thanks for everything.

(Katie exits. Travis listens for the French doors to close. He then goes to the CD player and turns on some music, listens and sways to the music for a moment, and goes back to preparing his salad.)

NICKY: *(Through the doors singing out.)* I'm hoooome.

TRAVIS: *(Warmly.)* I knooooow.

(Nicky enters carrying a little shopping bag. She sets it down, removes her coat, and hangs it on the hall tree.)

TRAVIS: *(Playfully.)* Come over here.

(Nicky goes over to Travis and snuggles in next to him.)

TRAVIS: You sure smell sexy.

NICKY: Oh, everything looks wonderful. And my favorite salad dressing. Can I have a bite?

TRAVIS: No. It's not finished. I'm still tossing. And I haven't added the avocado yet.

(Nicky sneaks a bite.)

TRAVIS: I saw that! *(He gives her a pat on her derrière.)* Bull's eye.

(Nicky gives him a peck on the back of the neck.)

NICKY: Now, you're going to smell like my favorite salad dressing all evening. Do you like my new dress?

TRAVIS: Let me see. *(Travis takes his hand and slides it down her hip.)* Hmmm. Satin. Let me guess. Blue. Sky blue.

NICKY: Yesss. And I had my hair done. Feel.

(Travis runs his fingers through her hair and inhales the pleasant fragrance.)

TRAVIS: You smell like gardenias.

NICKY: Really?

(He lifts her hair off the back of her neck and kisses her neck.)

TRAVIS: Don't move an inch. I'll be right back. I have something for you. *(Travis starts for the bedroom. He trips over a chair, manages to recover, slides the chair to its proper place, and without missing a step exits to the bedroom.)*

NICKY: *(To Travis in the bedroom.)* Damn her. Katie was here today. She knows that chair doesn't go there. I knew something looked different in here. Sometimes I think she does things on purpose. Half the time, I can't find what I'm looking for. I know she hides things.

(Travis enters the kitchen, takes the chair, and with one hand slides it over to the island. He puts a present on the table, swings the

chair around, straddles it, and effortlessly takes an apple from the fruit bowl and starts to eat it.)

TRAVIS: It's OK. It's not a big deal. So I tripped. People who can see trip all the time. I didn't hurt myself. Did I look funny? It breaks me up when I hear you trip. I imagine you looking very funny with those long legs of yours. And you think some imaginary thing has tripped you. Of course, it's not funny if you hurt yourself. *(Pause.)* What's on your mind? Why are you so angry?

NICKY: I'm not angry. I know she does things on purpose, that's all. She's a bitch!

(Travis sets the apple down, stands up, and continues to prepare the salad.)

TRAVIS: What else do I smell on you? At first I thought it was Max, your hairdresser. That can happen. But it's been more frequent lately. They say people want to get caught.

NICKY: People?

TRAVIS: Is it serious?

NICKY: Sometimes you're so . . . such a know-it-all. You think you've got this sixth sense or something.

TRAVIS: Yeah, I do about some things. But that has nothing to do with being blind. That's what happens when you love somebody . . . So what's up?

(Pause.)

NICKY: *(Gently.)* It's Johnny. He wants to get back together.

TRAVIS: Do you love him?

NICKY: No . . . yes. Actually, it's Natalie. I don't think she's adjusted to having a Sunday dad.

TRAVIS: Give them more time together. Let her stay with him the whole weekend. *(Pause.)* This has nothing to do with you? What about your needs? Natalie seems OK.

NICKY: I know. Natalie adores you. Travis, this has nothing to do with you and me. We need our family back together again . . . Natalie and me. This will all work out. Anyway, it's our anniversary today . . . Six months. Let's not spoil it. Let's have our dinner. OK? I have something for you, too.

(Nicky starts to walk toward the little table, as Travis reaches out and takes her hand. She turns to him.)

TRAVIS: I'll make it easy for you. I'll go take a walk. You can gather up some of your things while I'm gone. I'll help you carry them to your car when I get back. *(Travis goes to the table, retrieves his cell phone, takes his jacket from the hall tree, picks up his cane, and turns to Nicky.)* Will I be able to see you and Natalie occasionally? I'd like that.

NICKY: Of course. We'll just need a little time though.

TRAVIS: I know. I'll be cool. *(Holding up his cell phone.)* Call me when you're ready, and I'll get back here to help you carry your things out. *(Travis leaves.)*

THE TOPANGA RANCH MOTEL

(2 males/2 females, comedy)

BREAKDOWN Two couples from Oklahoma are vacationing in Malibu, California. They have just finished eating at The Reel Inn—a local fish place.

SETTING Bungalow at the Topanga Ranch Motel, Malibu, California.

• • •

(Wanda enters the bungalow first, carrying a sack of groceries. She is wearing a hot pink T-shirt with "Oklahoma Sooners" printed across the front, jeans, and sandals. Her husband, Wade, follows her. He's wearing a Hawaiian shirt, bathing trunks, sneakers, and socks. He is followed by Jackie wearing a bikini with a sarong tied around her waist, beads, and sandals. Joe, her husband—the last to enter—is wearing a T-shirt that says "Malibu," jeans, and a cowboy hat and boots. Wanda begins putting away the groceries in their kitchenette.)

JOE: I don't believe we had to stand in a long line like that . . . jest fer some fixins! How long did we have to wait?

WANDA: I don't know! But it sure waddn't worth it.

JACKIE: My catfish was great!! Jest like home.

WANDA: My supper was jest OK . . . I'm sorry I let that hippie girl talk me into those crab cakes. Yuck.

JOE: The seafood tacos sure sucked! I'm not even sure that's what it was. We've gotta find a good Mexican restaurant somewhere.

WANDA: I heard somebody mention that there was a Taco Bell up the road a piece.

WADE: Well, we've been here three days, and I haven't had any decent fixins yet.

JOE: Well, I'm hungry. Let's have some of those chips.

JACKIE: Would y'all all jest stop complainin'!

WADE: I can't believe it! It's June and it's freezin' out here! Sunny California—Ha! I can't believe this . . . .three days and look . . . I'm LOSIN' my suntan. Hey what's this? *(Wade opens his shirt exposing his chest to the threesome.)* Oh, great! Now what? Look, honey, I've got some kinda rash comin' on my chest. Now, I'm really gonna be miserable.

WANDA: Oh no, honey. Lemme see.

(Wade exits to the bathroom. Jackie is arranging her hair at the mirror.)

JACKIE: My. My. My. Complain. Complain. Complain. Now I've jest about had it with all the complainin'!

JOE: Ooooh Kaaaay. Who wants a beer?

JACKIE, WANDA: *(In unison.)* We do!

WADE: *(From the bathroom.)* Did anybody bother to pack a first-aid kit . . . or some Calamine lotion?

(The group doesn't respond. Wade peers out from the bathroom.)

WADE: Don't all y'all jump at once.

(Joe takes some cards out of his duffel bag.)

JOE: The girls can go get you some Calamine lotion next door at that little market. Why don't we play some cards while they're gone. How 'bout poker?

WANDA: Nooo . . . y'all play sumpin' we can play too.

(Wade enters from the bathroom.)

WADE: What? Hearts? Go fishin'? *(He laughs and makes a little snort.)*

JACKIE: I know! Let's play Cut the deck!

WANDA: Yeah! That's a great idea! Cut the deck!

(Joe pulls out a chair, sits at the Formica table, and starts to shuffle.)

JOE: Cut the what? What's that?

(Wanda sits at the table and takes the deck of cards from Joe.)

WANDA: Here, let me splain how we do it. OK. Now. Let's see . . . We shuffle the cards—reeeal good—then each player gets to cut the deck. The one with the lowest number wins a quarter!

(Jackie quickly joins Wanda at the table.)

JACKIE: Aces are high.

(Wade and Joe look at each other, roll their eyes, and snicker.)

WADE: That is totally retarded. Why don't you girls just go play jacks or somethin'. *(Wade sits down at the table.)*

WANDA: Oh, forget it! Just forget it! C'mon Jackie, let's go find some movie stars.

(Jackie takes a big swig of her beer.)

JACKIE: We could play staa-rrrip deck.

(The three look at her for a moment and glare. She takes another swig.)

WADE: What deck?

JOE: What's that?

JACKIE: Strip deck.

WANDA: Here, I'll show you. Gimme back the cards. OK, now here we go. First, we shuffle the deck reeeel good . . .

JACKIE: Then each person gets to cut the deck. The one who gets the lowest card has to take somethin' off.

JOE: Whooaa! I'm down!

WADE: Yep, that's a plan. Y'all can cut me in.

(The men click their bottles. Wanda shuffles the cards. She shuffles, and continues to shuffle. She shuffles some more.)

WADE, JACKIE, JOE: *(In unison.)* OK—that's got it!

(Wanda cuts the deck, then slowly peeks at her hand.)

WANDA: Seven a hearts! *(Wanda jumps up, does a little hip grind, and dances around her chair.)*

JACKIE: Go Wanda! Go Wanda!

WADE: Go girl! Look at my little sweetie pie!

(Wade laughs and snorts and scratches his chest. Wanda sits down and passes the deck to Wade. Joe glares at Jackie as Wade slowly cuts the deck.)

WADE: Queeen . . . of . . . hearts! *(Wade suddenly jumps up, grinds his hips, waves his arms, dances around, and tries to moonwalk.)* I am soooo bad!

JACKIE: Then get down with your bad self!!

WANDA: Go baby! That's my man.

JACKIE: Go Wade! Go Wade!

(Both women start to dance and grind with each other and Wade. Joe sits alone at the table glaring at the threesome.)

JOE: OK, settle down! You're acting like a bunch of fools! It's my turn!

JACKIE: Yeah. OK. All y'all settle down now. It's Joe's time.

(Joe takes the deck and quickly cuts it.)

JOE: Ace of spades.

(Wade laughs and snorts, coughs, and beats on the table. Joe hands the deck to Jackie looking at her with a threatening glare. Wade laughs and snorts again. Joe quickly looks at Wade and glares. Wade stops abruptly. Jackie slowly cuts the deck, peeks at the card, pauses, looks at the group, and smiles.)

JACKIE: Tooooo of spades.

(Joe suddenly jumps up.)

JOE: Wade, you were right. THIS IS TOTALLY RETARDED!

JACKIE: Joe, will you stop it! You're acting like a baby! *(Jackie stands up, slowly and seductively unties her sarong, and lets it drop to the floor.)*

WANDA: Go Jackie! Go Jackie!

(Joe walks over to Wanda, pulls off one of her sandals, and throws it on the floor. There is a long silence. Wade walks over to Jackie, takes off one of her sandals, and throws it on the floor. Joe takes his arm and wipes it across the table sending all the cards and beer bottles crashing to the floor. He turns and grabs a plastic picnic knife off the counter and points it threateningly at the threesome.)

JOE: Somebody's about to get hurt!

(The three crowd into a corner.)

WADE: Hey cowboy . . . take it easy. Now that's just not how the horse rode.

JOE: Hey, can't y'all take a joke . . . I've jest had a little too much to drink—that's all. OK? . . . Right. I'm outta here.

(Joe backs out through the door and disappears. Wanda and Wade sigh with relief. Wanda then starts to clean up.)

JACKIE: I'd better go get him. He jest got his feelins hurt that's all.

TOP SECRET

(1 male/1 female, drama)

BREAKDOWN Fay and Roy are brother and sister. Roy is in the military. He has just returned home from Iraq.

SETTING The living room belonging to Fay's and Roy's father.

• • •

(Fay is sitting in her father's living room looking through some old photographs. She is startled by the sound of a key opening the front door. The door opens slowly. Her brother Roy is standing in the doorway. He is wearing a military uniform.)

FAY: Oh . . . You still have a key.

ROY: Yeah . . . that's right . . . he's my dad, too.

FAY: Your dad? You haven't been around much lately.

ROY: How would you know?

FAY: I know!

ROY: Why are you so angry? The last time I was here—for the record—he was so drunk the whole time, I'm sure he didn't remember that I had even been here. He almost choked to death on his vomit. I had to take him to the hospital. I got him a nurse to live here—Rhoda. Where is she?

FAY: When was that?

ROY: A while ago. Why?

FAY: I've been trying to find you. And as usual "top secret"!

ROY: Stop raising your voice. He doesn't need to hear us fighting down here. Now, if I'm dismissed, I'm going upstairs to see him. *(Roy salutes her, and starts up the stairs.)*

FAY: You should let people know how to find you. It doesn't make any difference now anyway . . . He's dead.

(There is a long pause. Roy looks up toward their father's bedroom and then back to Fay.)

ROY: Dead? . . . Dad's dead? . . . Are you sure? . . . I mean . . . I mean . . . when did this happen? How? What happened? His nurse knows how to find me. Why didn't someone contact me? When did this happen?

FAY: The nurse is long gone . . . He took his life. He took some pills. Here . . . there's a note. He wrote it to you.

ROY: When did this happen?

FAY: A couple weeks ago. *(Fay starts to cry.)*

ROY: Why didn't someone try to find me? Was there a funeral?

FAY: No, he didn't want anything like that.

(Roy takes the note and opens it.)

FAY: I tried to find you! As usual, nobody could find you.

ROY: *(Roy reads.)* Dear Roy, I love you dearly, and I am very proud of you. I can no longer be a burden to you and Fay. Please take good care of her. By the way, I would like to be cremated. So long, Dad. *(A pause.)* What about his house?

FAY: I thought you might grieve at least a day maybe. You're really something.

ROY: I've had just about enough of your attitude . . . your holier-than-thou attitude.

FAY: The house is for sale—you'll get your share, don't worry.

ROY: I don't care about that! *(Quietly.)* I just need a place to stay for a while.

(Fay gets up and starts to the door.)

ROY: I have cancer. It's a brain tumor. I have to start treatments tomorrow. I'll be real sick. I was planning to stay with Dad while I was going through this. In the meantime, I was given a medical discharge. By the way, where are his ashes? You can put my urn next to his. Ha, ha.

(Fay slowly turns from the door. She is stunned.)

FAY: How can you joke about that?! My God! Oh, my God! I am so sorry. Oh, Roy. I am so sorry. When did you find out about this? What can I do?

ROY: A couple months ago. I found out while I was in Iraq. It's taken me this long to get through all the paperwork. I need you, Fay.

FAY: I'll be here. I promise you. You're gonna kick this, you'll see.

ROY: I know . . . Hey, I'm sorry I'm always so hard to find.

ROY, FAY: *(In unison.)* Top Secret.

ROY: How about you? I haven't asked. How are you doing?

FAY: I'm holding up. It's been real hard though.

ROY: What have you got here? Looks like some old pictures.

FAY: Roy, Roy . . .

ROY: I'm gonna lick this. I promise.

(Roy picks up a picture.)

ROY: Look at that. We were kinda cute then.

(Fay walks over and picks up the picture.)

FAY: Me, maybe . . . You were kind of funny looking.

(They hug.)

WILD FLOWERS

(1 male/1 female, drama)

BREAKDOWN Frances and Nolan have been married for three years.
Today is their anniversary.

SETTING The living room of the couple's penthouse.

• • •

*(Nolan is sitting on the sofa in the living room reading a letter.
He hears the sound of a key at the front door. It's his wife, Frances.
He quickly and neatly folds the letter and places it in his wallet.
Frances notices his awkwardness as she enters with a sack of gro-
ceries and some fresh flowers.)*

NOLAN: *(Brightly.)* Hi.

FRANCES: Hi.

(They give each other a quick little kiss.)

NOLAN: You're home early.

FRANCES: Not really.

NOLAN: Here, let me help you.

*(Nolan takes the groceries and starts into the kitchen. Frances enjoys
the fragrance of the fresh flowers.)*

FRANCES: What's up?

NOLAN: Nothing.

(Frances removes her coat.)

FRANCES: Could you bring me the green vase when you come
back in please. And put some water in it.

NOLAN: Sure.

(Nolan returns with the vase.)

FRANCES: Thanks, honey. *(She arranges the flowers in the vase.)* I'm sick of winter. I wanted to make the place look like spring-time. Mmm . . . they smell wonderful. They're beautiful, aren't they? They look like wild flowers.

(Nolan leans in to smell the flowers.)

NOLAN: Mmm . . . Yes, they do; they smell good.

FRANCES: *(Playfully.)* You've never done that before.

NOLAN: What?

FRANCES: *(Playfully.)* Smelled flowers. You never want to smell flowers. You hate strong fragrances. What was that you were hiding in your wallet when I came in?

NOLAN: What are you talking about?

FRANCES: *(Playfully.)* Don't play dumb. I saw you. You looked like you were hiding something in your wallet.

NOLAN: Don't play dumb? Look, I don't need this right now. Why are you always trying to start something?

FRANCES: Why are you being so defensive? What's the big deal? If you're not hiding anything, give me your wallet.

NOLAN: Sure! Come here and look. See? Driver's license, credit cards . . . business cards, money . . . You want some money? Here.

FRANCES: Sure I'll take the money and the wallet. *(She grabs the wallet finds the letter and waves it in the air.)* Ah-ha . . . I knew it!

(Nolan collapses onto the sofa.)

FRANCES: May I read it?

NOLAN: No! It's not yours.

FRANCES: OK . . . here . . . you read it. What does it say? What's the big secret?

NOLAN: It's a letter from Judi.

FRANCES: Judi? *(Frances sits down next to Nolan on the sofa. She opens the letter and reads it aloud.)* "Dear Nolan, Surprise! You haven't heard from me in a long time. I hope you and Frances are doing OK." *(Frances rolls her eyes.)* "I have something I've been meaning to tell you. We have a child." *(Frances turns and looks at Nolan.)* We have . . . a child? *(She continues to read.)* "She's four years old. Her name is Daisy. She's beautiful. She's smart and she's very sweet. I was going to keep this a secret from you forever, but now I decided that it would not be fair to Daisy. She needs her daddy, and deserves her daddy. So I'm asking you to meet with us and start to take a role in her life. I know that this will be a shock to you, and to Frances as well, but I also know the depth of your sensitivity. Enclosed is a picture of Daisy. Everybody thinks she looks like me." *(Frances looks at the picture, and then continues to read.)* "It was taken this past week on her birthday. I look forward to hearing from you. Sincerely, Judi P.S. Here is my phone number."

FRANCES: How do you know that this isn't a big lie?

NOLAN: I don't know.

FRANCES: What are you going to do about this?

NOLAN: I don't know. I mean, if I'm her . . . if she's my child, I intend to take this very seriously.

FRANCES: Well, do I have a choice here? I mean, does it matter how I might feel about this?

NOLAN: Yes, it matters. Just let me get myself together here—OK? And for once, think of someone other than yourself.

FRANCES: Screw you!

NOLAN: Nice talk!

(Frances starts to get up.)

NOLAN: Please, I'm sorry. Please . . . You know I didn't mean it. OK? Just . . . help me out here. I'm not your enemy. Help me to figure this out. What are we going to do?

FRANCES: I don't know. We'll call her tomorrow. I'm right here with you no matter what. You know that.

NOLAN: I know.

FRANCES: By the way . . .

NOLAN: What?

FRANCES: Nothing. I love you.

NOLAN: I love you, too. I didn't forget. Happy anniversary.